Praise for *Coac...*

Many coaching books merely skim the surface when it comes to the depth of work needed to become better leaders and people. Coaching For Powerful Change is cut from a different cloth. Each chapter invites you to reflect on your own choices and behavior so that you can make wise and informed decisions about how to become your best self.

Robert "Jake" Jacobs
Author, Real Time Strategic Change and
You Don't Have to Do It Alone

Coaching for Powerful Change opened my eyes - wide - on ways to transcend limitations and fears. Experienced life and career coaches give counsel through self-revealing questions, practical advice, and in many cases, step-by-step instructions. Discover self-illumination with a veritable dream team of advisors.

Suzette Martinez Standring,
Syndicated columnist and Award winning author of,
The Art of Column Writing and The Art of Opinion Writing

Coaching for Powerful Change is THE Yoga book of Coaching. Yoga says Sivananda is the art and science of becoming happy, perfect and realization of the self. Coaching is the facilitation for such. The day of the expert guru is gone. Today is the age of coaching others to be their own guru.

Roland Sullivan, Sullivan Transformation Agents
An orginal 100 Change Agent

COACHING FOR POWERFUL CHANGE

THE KEYS TO UNLOCKING PERSONAL AND PROFESSIONAL TRANSFORMATION

14 Business and Life Coaches Share Wisdom and
Inspiration to Create Life-Changing Transformation

Compiled by Diane E. Hayden, PhD
Foreword by Kelley Biskupiak, MA, CPCC and
Deb Elbaum, MD, CPCC, ACC

Natural Nutmeg Press, LLC
Avon, CT

ISBN: 978-0-9912600-2-7 (softcover)   ISBN: 978-0-9912600-3-4 (ebook)

Jacket & Interior Design by Chris Hindman.

Coaching for Powerful Change is available for bulk purchase, special promotions, and premiums. For pricing contact Diane@naturalnutmeg.com.

Publisher's Cataloging-In-Publication Data
(Prepared by The Donohue Group, Inc.)

Coaching for powerful change : the keys to unlocking personal and
  professional transformation : 14 business and life coaches share wisdom
  and inspiration to create life-changing transformation / compiled by
  Diane E. Hayden, PhD ; foreword by Kelley Biskupiak, MA, CPCC and Deb
  Elbaum, MD, CPCC, ACC.

    pages : illustrations ; cm

    Includes index.
    Issued also as an ebook.
    ISBN: 978-0-9912600-2-7 (softcover)

    1. Change (Psychology) 2. Self-realization. 3. Personal coaching. 4. Stress management. 5. Spiritual life. I. Hayden, Diane E. II. Biskupiak, Kelley. III. Elbaum, Deb.

BF637.C4 C53 2015
158.1

DISCLAIMER NOTE TO READER

This book is dedicated to those who have helped us on our journeys and to those who are beginning their own journey of transformation toward more happiness, purpose, and fulfillment. Know that the first step begins with a thought...that you can do this... and ends with the belief...that you have already accomplished it.

Table of Contents

Chapter 5

Chapter 6

Chapter 7

Chapter 8

Chapter 9

Chapter 10

The Hunger to Be a Leader

Tom Bohinc, MBA, CPCC

Chapter 11

Make the Connection

The Power of Vulnerability Every Man Should Know

Jeff Govoni, PCC

Chapter 12

Let it Go

Get Ready to Stretch, Grow and Move Forward

Heidi Werther, MS, CPCC, ACC

Chapter 13

Change....A Journey of Hope and Healing

Jeanne C. Zuzel, RN, MA

Chapter 14

Tending To Our Inner World To Create Better Results In Our Outer World

Lynnea Brinkerhoff, MSOD, PCC

Epilogue

Foreword

Imagine this book as an invitation -- your invitation to a Bigger Life. A More Meaningful Life. A Happier, Healthier Life. "Sign me up!" you say.

Then the doubts creep in. You might hear critical voices in your head saying things like: What makes you think you can change? How do you even know what you want? Do you even have time in your busy life to focus on making a change?

To all of those doubts, we state unequivocally: You CAN do it. It is YOUR time. We want to watch you shine. A life filled with purpose, meaning, and happiness is what you are here to live. We believe this book sitting in your hands is a tool to help you get there.

Business and life coaching has exploded over the last decade. For-profit and non-profit companies alike have embraced leadership coaching. Coaching has been incorporated into educational institutions. On an individual level, life coaching helps people find more meaning and balance in their lives. However, it is important to know what coaching is, why you might want to work with a coach, where to find a quality coach, and what benefits to expect from coaching. Let's explore a few of these questions.

What is a coach?

There are many definitions, ideas, and thoughts swimming around out there, but for the coaches contributing to this book, we look at our role very simply: we are your fearless and compassionate partners. We are there to walk by your side, ask powerful questions, cheer you on, encourage you to take risks, and champion you to live your best life, both personally and professionally. We are not afraid to hold you accountable for accomplishing goals and benchmarks you set for yourself, and we are willing to navigate deep emotions that bubble up as we walk this road with you.

We have a variety of tools, techniques, and structures -- many that you will find in this book -- to guide you through the process of transformation. However, the "work" is for you to do. We will not solve your problems or make your decisions for you. We believe this journey is yours. Our role is to help you unlock the pieces of who you are that will propel you toward the life you truly want to be living.

Why might you seek out coaching?

There are a variety of reasons you may seek out coaching. Here are a few examples:
• When you are looking to expand or grow an area of your life
• When you are navigating a professional or personal transition
• When you are searching for more clarity, confidence, vision, and direction
• To gain more balance and fulfillment

Does coaching work?

YES! We believe strongly in the coaching relationships we have cultivated over the years. Our clients' testimonials support this. The results are tangible and intangible. Clients become happier, less stressed, and make decisions with more clarity and intention. They also get new jobs, increase leadership skills, grow businesses, become healthier, and find new relationships.

Where can I find a quality, experienced coach?

The International Coach Federation (ICF) is one place to start. These coaches have all completed an in-depth body of study, logged hours with multiple clients, and have been tested on a code of ethics around the coaching relationship. Other places to find a coach include ICF-certified coaching schools and programs, such as Coaches Training Institute (CTI), CoachU, and IPEC. You can also reach out to coaches in this book. As you read through the chapters, ask yourself, "Does this coach really speak to me?" If the answer is YES, contact him or her and set up an appointment.

****

Let's talk about how you can make this book work for you. All of the coaches who have contributed to this book have helped clients create intentional change in their lives. As coaches, we have been privileged to walk the journey of transformation with our clients. We have had front row seats to the unfolding of the process of change. We want to be clear: transformation is a journey and a process. Sometimes it moves at warp speed, and other times it inches along slowly.

As we grow and change, we experience peaks and valleys. We all have moments when we feel all-powerful and invincible. We feel like we can take on the world. Conversely, we all have times when we feel stuck in our lives. We might experience frustration, sadness, and pain. These are times when some of our deepest learning and growth takes place. Looking at our lives honestly to see what is working well and what isn't working well takes courage and bravery. Claiming the change we want for ourselves, and then taking action to move forward demands strength, dedication, and vulnerability.

Here's what we want you to know: all of the authors in this book are enthusiastically rooting for you. We are on your team, cheering you on, holding the vision you want for your life, and believing in you. We invite you to believe in yourself. We ask that you be willing to try something new, by putting one foot in front of the other. Transformation is yours for the taking.

What we love about this book is that each chapter provides real, accessible, do-able exercises and tools you can employ and put into action right away. When you read this book and engage in the exercises, you will create intentional changes. Shifts will begin to happen.

There are different ways to use this book. You can start at the beginning and read the chapters straight through. Or you can see which chapter titles and topics grab your immediate attention. You can do the exercises as you read each chapter, or you can read the chapters first and then return later to the exercises that intrigue you most.

Choose the approach that fits you best, and do it with intention. Some chapters speak generally to topics we can all relate to. These include taking the time to stop and pause in our busy lives, readying ourselves for change, and seeking purpose and authenticity in our lives. Other chapters discuss a wide variety of focused topics, such as nourishing our spiritual life, examining our relationship to our finances, creating meaningful relationships, seeking a job purposefully, and claiming our own leadership. We even have a chapter directed toward men (and the people who love them) about the power of vulnerability. Some chapters will resonate with you today. Others will be more relevant at other times in your life. Yet, all of the chapters are based on the common thread of evoking transformation.

Let's get started! Find yourself a comfy place to sit, and grab a pen and journal. We invite you to start with these questions:

What's the cost to you (emotionally, professionally, financially) if nothing changes in your life?
What could be possible if you were able to make a change?
What might your life look like one year from now?
Five years from now? Ten years from now?

Think about that for a minute or two. Let your mind dream about the possibilities. Turn the page. The journey awaits.

Kelley Biskupiak, MA, CPCC, and
Deb Elbaum, MD, CPCC, ACC
August, 2015

Chapter 1

Giving New Meaning to "ME-Time"
Mindset Tips for You to Ignite
Living Your Best Life

Kelley Biskupiak, MA, CPCC

**In a world where there is no rest,
we must find space for what renews our soul.**
- Ian Stephenson

This quote is the foundation of my coaching practice, workshops and public speaking. We have created and are living in a day and age where there is no rest. We have become masters at doing. Many of us could have earned our PhD in multitasking at this point in the game. Our to-do lists are long and full and I am fairly certain there is not a to-do item that says, "Take some--ME-time." As women we are masters at putting ourselves on the backburner in service of everyone and everything around us. We often act as the visionaries for those we love the most but in making this choice we miss out on being our own visionaries. There is a very harsh reality to all of this doing playing out in the world. In the process of living these jam-packed lives we are losing ourselves. We are losing the very best parts of who we are and, most importantly, we are losing the opportunity to show up and REALLY live life. I am here to tell you living this way is a choice and you can choose differently right here and now. I believe this chapter will challenge you to reconstruct the way you create "Me-Time" in your life and ignite you into living your best life!

Let's get started shall we?

I look at my job in a very simple way. My title is Personal and Professional Life Coach, but I am a space creator. Yes, that simple...a space creator. I create space for women to slow their lives down and focus on exactly who they are and what they want from their lives. The power and impact that occurs when you give a woman time to really fill herself back up is nothing short of miraculous. When a woman knows who she is and what her purpose is, the world becomes better because of it. Period.

In the work that I do women often come to me seeking more balance or fulfillment. They usually show up in one of two ways:

My life is utter chaos. My brain is so full it might explode. I run from thing to thing not 100% clear how I even got so much on my plate, and most days I feel exhausted and depleted. I want off of this treadmill. How do I balance everything?

OR

I have it all. Every box is checked:
- ✔ *The career*
- ✔ *The partner*
- ✔ *The family*
- ✔ *The friends*
- ✔ *The status*

For all intents and purposes my life is beautiful...but I have a secret (one that often I feel great shame about). I am not happy. I don't feel fulfilled. As a matter of fact, I don't really feel much of anything anymore. Is there more for me?

These two ways of being are created by a series of stories or mindsets that do not serve to fuel your life. We are going to explore and deconstruct the top three Mindset Myths that you can start letting go of to begin to fuel up your life starting today.

Mindset Myth One:
I'll be enough when I...
Lose 10 lbs., get more organized, land that big job, have that baby, buy the big house, marry that partner

Mindset Shift:
No! You are enough right now!

It is understandable that this "not enough" mindset myth exists as we live in a day and age fueled by media images and social media outlets that are underpinned by threads of comparison. However, there is an extreme danger and cost to operating in this mindset. Your unique talents and gifts are at stake. When operating in this mindset we slowly start to let go of whom it is that we truly are...in place of whom it is we feel others think we should be. These perceptions, standards or stories we create begin to run our lives in a way that is both exhausting and depleting.

How many of you feel stressed, exhausted and less than adequate when holiday cards come out and you have yet to get that perfect shot of your family? How often do you hop onto a social media site and see the amazing vacation your friend from high school is on in Aruba, and you can barely make your mortgage payment?

Do you get triggered when you get a request from the room mother to volunteer at your child's class party, but you have 3 days of travel for work and you know you can't be there? It may be that you have been a stay-at-home mother for the last 5 years and everyone around you is heading back to work and you don't have a clue what is next for you. It could be that you see the ladies walking around town who frequent Boot Camp, slim and fit donning a tight pair of Lulu-lemon yoga pants and you have not seen the inside of a gym in years.

You all have your own version of how this plays out in your life. I want you to notice what you think and say to yourself when this comes up in your life.

What perceptions, standards or stories am I creating? Are they living in the land of, "I am not enough?"

Dr. Brene Brown, a leading research professor at the University of Houston Graduate College of Social Work states, "Perceptions dictate how you feel, think and behave everyday." Knowing this truth is the key to combatting the "not enough" mindset.

You must examine your perceptions, standards and stories

Very simply, not doing this will cost you the fuel you need to propel your life toward more of what you truly want. You CAN change your perceptions, standards or stories but you MUST know them and understand them first. Let's walk through some powerful questions you can use to examine your perceptions and work towards freeing yourself from the "not enough" mindset myth.

❖ What gets me triggered? What sends me into that place of not feeling like I am enough? List or write down a place or places in your life when this happens.

❖ Ask yourself: **How do I want to be perceived?**
   I want to be viewed this way_____.

❖ Ask yourself: **How I DO NOT** want to be perceived?
   I DO NOT want to be viewed this way_____.

❖ How much time and energy am I spending trying to hustle and control this in my life? What is the cost of that? What are people missing about who I really am in the process?

❖ Review each point above. **Is this what I really want for my life?** If it is, examine it just a little more.
   1. Is it linked to an ideal vision you have created?
   2. Does this come from some standard that was set in your childhood? If so, does it still make sense in the present day?
   3. Is it linked to being perfect or imperfect?
   4. Is it how you hustle to be loved or to be lovable?

After all of this exploring, complete the following statement:

This is how I want to view this in my life going forward…

Using this process will get you very clear about what system you are operating from and the perceptions that are fueling or blocking you from what you really want for your life. This is an excellent exercise to walk yourself through and then discuss with a coach or mentor.

When we begin to see ourselves from a place of enough, huge shifts happen. We go after more of what we want from a place of confidence and employ self-compassion when things do not go our way. Loving exactly who you are today is crucially important in living your best life. We are human, we make mistakes and some days we are AMAZING and other days we might just BOMB completely, but no matter what we are ENOUGH.

~You are enough~

Mindset Myth Two:
Putting myself last is what is right, honorable or just the way it has to be.

Mindset Shift:
Your self-care is not a luxury, it is a necessity!

This mindset myth is killing the talent, the gifts, the creativity and the power of women on a daily basis. It is that clear-cut. I see it in the clients I work with, in the women who attend my workshops and also in most conversations I have with women. Living with this mindset myth is a lie that women tell themselves. You see, when you live in a place of constant deprivation in sacrifice of everyone around you; you are giving them a depleted, exhausted version of who you really are.

Consider this, the speech they give you on an airline flight before you taxi down the runway is, "Put on your oxygen mask first. Then assist those around you." The reason behind this safety procedure is that you are no use to your children, your spouse, your elderly parents or your neighbors if you're not breathing yourself. Let's take that logic and apply it here. You are not doing anyone any favors if you are operating on too little life oxygen. If you are empty then everyone around you suffers because you are keeping them from the true greatness you have to offer. You may be able to operate but at what cost? What is the cost to everyone around you? Your self-care is paramount in living your best life and I am not talking about a pedicure or a massage once in a while. There are very specific arenas of who you are that need to be filled in order to really fuel your life.

A strong self-care plan begins with understanding the four areas of your life that are the foundation from which your life fuel comes. These areas are mental, physical, spiritual and emotional. When you are depleted in any of these areas your life is impacted. Let's breakdown those areas and give you some tips to get you fueling yourself back up today!

Emotional ⬐ Mental ⬏

Physical ⬐

Self-care

Spiritual ⬏

What do I need?
Creating life fuel

Grab a journal and use this page as your guide to explore what you need right now to fuel your life.

STEP ONE
~ Consider these questions ~

- ✔ Where do I feel depleted or deprived?
- ✔ What do I need more of right now?
- ✔ What do I need less of?
- ✔ What do I want for myself?
- ✔ What am I craving more of in my life?
- ✔ Who or what is causing me to be resentful right now? What might be the cause of this?

STEP TWO
~ Review the four fuel areas ~

How do you care for yourself in each?
Brainstorm possible ways to refuel yourself.

Physically	Emotionally	Mentally	Spiritually
How do you care for yourself physically?	How do you care for yourself emotionally?	How do you care for yourself mentally?	How do you care for yourself spiritually?
New ideas or ways I want to try:	New ideas or ways I want to try:	New ideas or ways I want to try:	New ideas or ways I want to try:
Tips:	**Tips:**	**Tips:**	**Tips:**
* What foods energize you and make you feel great? Eat that!	* Have a "real" conversation with a good friend or mentor.	* Get reading that book you have wanted to or see that movie that you know will make you think.	* Make a date with yourself, just you and maybe a journal.
* Bring down your stress by exercising. It also replenishes your energy!	* Think only kind and loving thoughts about yourself! For one week make no negative judgments about yourself.	* Try something new that will challenge you.	* Take a walk outside, look around and notice the beauty.
* Getting proper sleep and staying hydrated to rejuvenate you. Take a nap or sleep in, and get a new water bottle.	* Find support from a coach, therapist, or counselor.	* Sign up for a class, group or workshop that catches your attention.	* Pray or download a new meditation application and create space to reflect and focus on gratitude.
* Pamper yourself. What makes you feel pampered? Do that!	* Plan a "girl's night out."	* Seek out opportunities in your community or at work that will make you learn something new.	* Get creative: paint, draw, dance, write, and sing.
	* Have a good cry and let yourself go. Then journal about it.		* Is there a cause you are passionate about? Volunteer!

STEP THREE
~ Grant Yourself Permission ~

The same love and compassion you give to others in your life is the same love and compassion you deserve and need to be giving to yourself. Often it begins by granting yourself permission to let go of the way you have viewed self-care. So often, my clients will talk about how they feel selfish for taking time out to care for themselves. One of the biggest leaps my clients make is in signing a contract with me. It is often a symbol of their declaration and commitment to their own self-care and it takes great courage to make that leap. Doing something differently than you have ever done before and making your own self-care a priority will mean letting others down or leaving them disappointed. The courage to stick with your self-care when you are letting others down is a challenge but one well worth the pain. Creating a strong self-care plan will assist you when these challenging points arise. You are worth it, you deserve it and the world will bene-fit from it. Now, I challenge you to make it happen!

~ Your self-care is not a luxury, it is a necessity ~

Mindset Myth Three:

I am a Perfectionist
I am a Pleaser
I am a Performer

Mindset Shift:
Permission to be you!

It is interesting that long before I knew the work of Brene Brown, I noticed a general trend happening with the women in my coaching sessions and also in workshops I both attended and facilitat-ed. Women were living out one or a combination of all three of these personas in their lives:

The Perfectionist: I will not let you see my flaws at any cost. I am completely in control of everything. If for some reason my flaws are exposed I will beat myself up for the missed details or employ the weapon of blaming others.

The Pleaser: I will please you no matter the cost to myself. I will say yes even when my plate is overflowing and I will NEVER step into a confrontational role...EVER! Resentment is my wingman.

The Performer: I will out perform everyone and everything. I will put on a spectacular show no matter the exhaustion and depletion this creates in my life.

All three live in the land of not wanting to fail, be judged or disappoint. These are brilliant mechanisms that we create to protect us from the pain that might be induced by failure, judgment and disappointment. However, somewhere along the way these mechanisms have stopped serving your life. They have become what holds you back and keeps you from living a balanced and fulfilled life. They also, and more dangerously, keep the world from really seeing who you are and the cost of that is true connection with others. Here is what I know. YOU are craving connection. You are hard wired for it and each time you block yourself (or protect yourself) from being seen you are moving your life further and further away from what you truly want.

I feel the best way to illustrate how this can play out in your life is from a real life example and that real life…is mine. You will have your own unique version of how this happens in your life but the following is a spotlight on how we can work our way through.

The scenario:

I was asked to do my first big workshop for a corporate women's leadership network…I calmly freaked. You know that silent freak-out you do:

"I can do this." "Wait, can I do this?" "I am not corporate!" "I have never even worked in corporate America!!" "Are they going to like my workshop?" "I don't know if I have what it takes." "OH MY GOD what did I get myself into!!!"

Fear, anxiety, limitations and self-doubt were running me. This launched me into PERFECTIONIST mode. I began to double, triple, and quadruple check my workbook for attendees, and nothing seemed good enough. I repeatedly practiced my speaking parts, judging and criticizing each and every mistake I made. That fear was growing and any mistake I made in the privacy of my own office felt like a noose of suffocation. The general feeling at this point was if I made one mistake in this workshop my career was over. Ahh! How could anyone perform under that pressure? Truth be told, long before this event my Little Miss Perfect persona had served me up some really big accomplishments and most were due to her performance. However, one issue remained…I was not "bringing" my whole self to the table. I was not giving myself permission to truly be me. There was this fake quality that I knew showed up. It did not matter if others knew this or not. I knew it and that mattered most. The truth for me was that long after the achievements and the accolades faded into the background, a sinking feeling that I still had not done enough would surface…a feeling that I was not enough. I was triggered…BIG TIME!

It was my awareness and recognition of this very personal truth that compelled me to go at this event differently! I walked myself through the entire gammit of Mindset Shifts One and Two. What were my perceptions? Where were they born? What did I truly want? How was I doing on self-care? What areas needed some attention and quickly? I talked with my husband, a colleague and my own professional coach. In my reflection it became very clear what permission I needed to employ to live this event differently.

I granted myself permission to mess up, fail out loud and roll with it unapologetically.
I granted myself permission to have FUN! I love this work that I do. It brings great joy to my life and I want to show-up and be there to experience it.
I granted myself permission to BE ME BRAVELY!

Here is what happened. What once would be seen as failures became learning opportunities. I learned so much from this experience and my workshop grew deeper and stronger because of it. I recognized more of the work I want to be doing and what I do not want to do. I felt the full joy of the experience. I recognized the privilege it is to be able to do this very personal work with people and very simply I had FUN! The most important piece in reflecting on this was that I filled that craving we all have for true connection. In showing up and owning all parts of myself I actually granted permission for the attendees to show-up and really own who they were during the workshop. Permission to be yourself became contagious!

You have 100% permission at all times to grant yourself the opportunity to show up as exactly who you are. Beautiful flaws, hard to say no's and acting classes all left behind. There is no one quite like you and whenever you make the choice to not show-up and "do" you the world dims a little bit. It is our willingness to fail out loud that makes transformation possible. It is where growth happens.

Try this Mindset Shift Challenge:

When this mindset creeps in. **STOP and notice what is happening**. *Make time to reflect on what is taking place and hit that Pause Button. Then try answering these powerful questions:*

- ✔ Where am I not granting myself permission?
- ✔ What story am I caught up in?
- ✔ What might change that?
- ✔ What do I really want for myself?
- ✔ What permission am I giving myself?

~ Permission to Be Me Bravely ~

NOW: I Challenge You!

We have looked at three mindsets myths that can keep you stuck or blocked from living your best life. I challenge you to take these mindset tips and create the kind of "Me-Time" in your life that is not only meaningful but necessary. You deserve to be living your best and it all begins with this:

~ Know who you are ~

This truth is the foundation of creating a life that is both full and balanced. Knowing all parts of who you are; the light, the dark, the messy and the clean are the key to fueling up your life.

And I am here to tell you…you must carve out time in your life to gain this clarity. It is crucial that you get clear about exactly who you are, what you want for your life and most importantly live it out in the world for all to see. This world needs everything you have to offer. So, I challenge you today and everyday to do the work it takes to live this one life you have been given as fully as you possibly can!

Uniquely qualified founder and owner of Be You Bravely, Kelley Biskupiak launched this personal and professional coaching firm because she believes strongly in empowering women and families to lead and live fulfilling lives. Kelley works with clients to get clarity in the chaos and develop a goal-based purpose plan that can be implemented into their life. The result is more balance and fulfillment and a life lived with purpose and meaning. As a wife, mother of three boys, business owner, Workshop Facilitator, Motivational Speaker, Blogger, Author and Educational Leadership Coach, Kelley has learned to "walk this talk" in her own life. Kelley holds a BA in both Communication Studies and Education, from the University of Rhode Island as well as a Masters Degree in Literacy from Pace University. She has worked in the educational arena in many capacities ranging from teaching, administration and consulting. She currently works for Leadership Greater Hartford as an Educational Leadership Coach and is Principal at her coaching practice, Be You Bravely. Kelley is also host and facilitator for a monthly workshop series for women titled, "Ladies Night Out." Kelley was trained as a Co-Active Coach at the esteemed Coaches Training Institute (CTI) and holds a CPCC certification. She is a member of the International Coaching Federation (ICF). Kelley Biskupiak, MA, CPCC, 203-216-3956, beyoubravely.com, kelley@beyoubravely.com.

Chapter 2

Making Moments Count
How to Recognize and
Claim Your Life Purpose

Deb Elbaum, MD, CPCC, ACC

After I graduated from medical school, I began my training to become a physician. I had always wanted to help others, and I believed this was the way I would do it. Soon after I began the training, I realized that despite my desire to connect with patients, the daily work was not for me. I dreaded emergencies, couldn't wait to leave after each shift, and developed an ulcer. I quit and entered a professional hibernation. For the next few years, I raised my children. I loved being with them, but always at the back of my mind was the thought, "Is this all there is?"

- Deb, age 45, coach

Here's what I believe: that you matter, and that you can contribute meaningfully to the people and world around you in a unique way. In other words, you have a purpose. Given that you are living and that you have a purpose, it seems reasonable to claim that you have a "life purpose."

Interestingly, though, most of the people I talk with don't initially relate to the term "life purpose." They believe that life purpose is a specific career or a lofty accomplishment that one aspires to achieve. When I interview people and ask them what life purpose means, they say:

"That's a loaded question. I think I'm a good person, but I don't have a life purpose."

"It's too big. It's not relatable."

"I don't feel yet like I am living my life purpose. I feel like it is somewhere

'out there'. I imagine that when I find my life purpose, things will be easy."

"It makes me think of a big accomplishment that is unattainable, like curing cancer."

After I ask people about their life purpose, I ask them about the phrase "living on purpose." People usually quickly respond, saying, "Oh, that is different." In contrast to life purpose, they see living on purpose as a reason one does certain daily activities.

It involves connecting with the meaning in life, whether at a job or volunteer position, with family or friends. When asked to define this phrase, people say:

"Living on purpose means something active, living moment by moment. It is in my grasp."

"It is being mindful and present, and interacting with people in that way."

"Living on purpose means being mindful, thoughtful, and conscious of what I am doing each day. It feels good."

"It's being intentional and looking back at the end of each day and not feeling wasteful."

Here's what you need to know, though: **life purpose and living on purpose are absolutely connected**. You can't have one without the other. They are both about you and how you interact with the world each day and during the years of your life. In fact, when I later question people about how life purpose and living on purpose are connected, they come to see a connection. They say:

"If I am living on purpose by being fulfilled in this moment, then I am living my life purpose."

"Living on purpose adds up to the sum of my life purpose."

"I can't do one without the other. If I am not mindful and living on purpose, then I am not living my life purpose."

"By verbalizing and vocalizing my life purpose, it allows me to live on purpose."

In this chapter, we will explore life purpose, what it means, how you can connect with your purpose, and how you can find more purpose in your daily life. My wish for you is that, by the end of this chapter, you will be able to answer the question, "How am I living purposefully today?"

You'll notice that I use the terms life purpose and living on purpose interchangeably in this chapter. That's a deliberate choice, to remind you that when you live on purpose, you are living your life purpose.

> ### *When you live on purpose, you are living your life purpose.*

What Does "Life Purpose" Mean, Anyway?

Life purpose is living in a way that feels alive, exciting, and meaningful. It means having a sense of your unique gifts and using them in a way that positively affects the people and world around you.

Life purpose is *not* a specific achievement or career title; it is also not one single thing. Life purpose is multidimensional and multi-faceted, similar to a diamond that has many sides. All of the sides of the diamond matter, as they all contribute to its brilliance. You can have a purpose professionally and within your family, as purpose is about your way of interacting with the world.

Life purpose can also evolve over time. Although aspects of your life purpose might be constant, the entirety of your life purpose can and will shift over time. As we continue to fine-tune our strengths and add to our knowledge about ourselves, what we enjoy, and what we are good at, our life purpose will deepen and become clearer.

A person's life purpose is also different than a life goal. Here's an example. Suppose your friend has been talking about climbing a mountain her whole life. You might wonder, "Wouldn't that be considered a life purpose?"

Although an impressive accomplishment, climbing that mountain would be a life goal. Life goals are often aligned with a person's life purpose and stem naturally when people live on purpose. Rather than achieving a goal, however, life purpose is how you live in the world.

For instance, this woman's life purpose might be championing others to take on challenges, being a passionate athlete, or advocating for the environment.

"My life purpose right now is to help people feel well and tap into their ability to heal themselves. My clients go out into the world as a beacon of health and happiness and inspire others. There's a trickle-down effect as their friends and family see that being healthy and happy is an option."
- Ann, age 47, Holistic Health and Wellness Coach

Why Talk about Life Purpose?

Recognizing and connecting with the purpose in your life is critical. Let's face it, many things in today's world are scary, overwhelming, and downright depressing. When you feel lost or unsure, your purpose can guide you. Knowing what drives you and what matters most can help you make choices about work, family, and life that are right for you.

You can think of your purpose like a hand-held metal detector you might see people using at a beach or in the woods to scan for objects buried under the ground. Just like a metal detector points you to possible buried treasure, your internal purpose guides you to conversations, activities, and work that are most meaningful to you.

When we have a sense of purpose in what we are doing or how we are being with others, we:

• Feel like our lives have more meaning and direction
• Are happier
• Are excited about our work
• Balance work and family life better
• Are kinder and more compassionate with ourselves and others

When we don't have a sense of purpose in what we are doing, and when we feel like what we are doing is pointless or unappreciated, we often:
• Feel resentful or depressed
• Are less compassionate with ourselves and others

- Spend a lot of time thinking about the past or worrying about the future
- Engage in mind-numbing activities, such as watching TV and surfing the internet
- Close ourselves off emotionally

> ***When you have purpose in your life, you are more likely to feel happier and kinder to yourself and others.***

Tools to Clarify Your Purpose

Now that we have talked about why purpose matters, it's time to start recognizing and claiming your life purpose. To help my clients get started, I like to use the Detective Approach. You know how detectives are really curious? It's time for you to get curious about your own life.

First, find a comfortable place where you can sit and write. You can write your answers in this book, in a journal, on your phone, or on your computer. You are going to play the role of detective and get curious about your life and what makes you tick. Most importantly, you are going to do this without judgment. This bears repeating:

You Are Not Allowed To Judge Yourself During These Exercises!

Ask yourself the following questions one at a time and write down your answers:

- When was a recent time that I felt excited and passionate about what I was doing?
- What was I doing?
- What part of this was most meaningful to me?
- What was the impact I had on the people or world around me?
- When I wake up in the morning, what I am excited to do?
- When does time seem to fly for me?
- What have I created in my life that I am proud of?

Great job! You are off to a solid start. After you have interviewed yourself, it is time to interview other people. Just like real detectives interview witnesses to get their points of view, you will get some different perspectives about your life.

Choose one or two people who know you well and with whom you would feel comfortable talking about these things. Call them or meet with them and ask the following questions. Be sure to write down the answers. Ask them:

- When do you see me being most excited and happy?
- What have I done that you admire?
- What do you appreciate about me?

"I left a job that was not life-giving for me and decided to take some time as a stay-at-home parent after having my first child. I am still on a journey to find out what my life purpose is. To figure it out, I use logic and facts, and I also listen to what my gut tells me. As I think about decisions I'm making or try new things, I ask myself, "Does this fit you? Is this who you are?"

- Lora, age 37, Stay-At-Home Parent

Claiming Your Purpose

It's time to review the information you have gathered from your investigating and imagining. Let's pretend all of this material you've gathered is "data." Just like scientists, let's review what you wrote down to see what jumps out at you.

- What patterns do you see in your data?
- What words came up over and over?
- What have you learned about what makes you feel purposeful?

Now, summarize your findings and fill in the following statement: I feel the most present, happy, excited, fulfilled, and purposeful when I _____.

"I started living life on purpose by being intentional…intentional with my words, with the food I was eating, with my relationships, and with exercise. By being intentional, I am present, and am much less likely to over-glorify the past or overanalyze the future. When I feel my thoughts start to spiral out of control, I capture that thought and replace it with one focusing on what I am grateful for right now in this moment."

- Elizabeth, age 25, Graduate Student and Fitness Instructor

Now What?

Hopefully by now you've learned something about your purpose…what lights you up and how you find meaning in your everyday life. You might be wondering, "What now?"

First, keep refining your purpose. Remember when I said that your purpose is constantly evolving? Action helps you find new things that you enjoy and are good at. A former client of mine said, "It's tough to figure out life by thinking. You need to dabble and become active to find out what you are passionate about." I completely agree! We learn about ourselves by stepping out of our comfort zone and trying new things.

Give yourself permission to try something completely new. You might sign up for a class that sounds interesting, start a blog and write your first blog post, volunteer in your community, or tag along with a friend to his or her favorite activity.

You can hold yourself accountable by choosing a date to complete this new thing by, and writing it in your calendar. Then, DO IT, have fun, and see what you learn about yourself.

> **Give yourself permission to try something completely new to learn more about you.**

Second, connect with the purpose in your day-to-day life. You can find purpose in your daily life, in the work and activities you do already. All this requires is that you be mindful and intentional. It requires you to pause and take stock during the day, to look at your life from a new perspective.

For example, let's say that genuine connections with others fill you with purpose. Where are the connections that you can deepen in your everyday life?

Every day, whether at work, or with family and friends, make an effort to pause a few times during the day. Look up from what you are doing and ask yourself, "How am I living purposefully right now?"

You might want to incorporate a daily practice of connecting with your purpose. Before you go to bed each night, ask yourself, "What's one way that I lived on purpose today?"

Ask yourself every day, "How did I live on purpose today?"

My Hope for You

It is my hope that you will grow to be more connected to the purpose in your life, and, consequently, to the thought that you matter deeply in this world. I believe that as you live more purposefully every day, you will feel happier, more fulfilled, and more connected to the people around you.

Living on purpose will create new pathways for your life that you haven't yet imagined. Purposeful living opens up your thinking to new ideas, new things to try, and new ways to be. And even though I don't know exactly what your future holds, I do know that when you consciously choose to claim the purpose in your life, exciting possibilities will open up. Enjoy the journey, as you see where your purpose takes you.

"After I left medicine, I built a career as a freelance writer. The work was fine, but it was not fulfilling. Eventually, I decided it was time to find more meaning in my life. A coach whom I admired encouraged me to sign up for coaching training. After the first weekend of classes, I was transformed. I reconnected with my desire to deeply connect with others. I learned that I am passionate about helping others recognize and harness their strengths. Now, every time I coach a client, I am living my life purpose."

- Deb, age 45, Coach

Deb Elbaum, MD, CPCC, ACC, is a certified career and life coach who helps her clients get clear about their choices, take action, trust their decisions, and create intentional change. She works with professionals who are navigating career transition, women who are reentering the workforce, and individuals who are seeking more purpose in life. Before becoming a coach, Deb worked as a physician and medical writer. In addition to being a coach, author, speaker, wife, and mother, Deb is a Founding Fellow at the Harvard Medical School-affiliated Institute of Coaching, a nonprofit organization dedicated to furthering quality research on coaching. She is also a coach and workshop presenter for the Institute for Career Transitions at Massachusetts Institute of Technology, an organization supporting long-term unemployed individuals. Her bachelor's degree in psychology is from Harvard University, her MD degree is from the University of Pennsylvania, and her coaching certification is from the Coaches Training Institute. She lives in Massachusetts with her husband and three children. For more information, visit www. DebElbaum.com or email Deb@DebElbaum.com.

Chapter 3

Nurturing Wellness from Within
Creating Positive HealthStyles through Integrative Health Coaching

Christel Autuori, RDH, RYT, MA

Are you feeling your best? Do you wake up every morning rested, energized, and eagerly anticipating a great day? Are you happy with your physical, mental, emotional, and spiritual self? Are you living and working in an environment that is comfortable, supportive and nurturing? Do you have a sense of satisfaction in your personal and professional life? Do you have a strong sense of community, of belonging to something bigger than yourself? Are you well nourished—physically, spiritually, culturally and emotionally? Do you challenge and exercise your mind as well as your body? Do you take time for yourself, or are you running from one event to another with barely a chance to breathe, never mind to stop and smell the flowers? In short, are you living the life you want…a life of vitality and optimal health?

Maybe you have wanted to make a change for a happier and healthier life, or have tried to make changes in the past but were not successful. You know yourself better than anyone. You know what is important to you, what motivates you, what makes you tick. You have inner strengths and experience that you can tap into and use to orchestrate, cultivate, and maintain the life of satisfaction, vitality, and well-being that you deserve.

The Integrative Approach

The integrative approach to health and healing is not new, and dates back to ancient times. Hippocrates (c. 460-c.370BC) is the classical Greek physician considered to be the "founder" of medicine, and for whom the Hippocratic Oath taken by physicians is named. Hippocrates took a holistic and integrative perspective to the practice of medicine, advocating the examination and observation of the patient in all systems; body, mind, and spirit. He believed in the innate healing power of nature, and that diseases were manifestations of imbalances in the system. Restore balance, restore health.

In 1946 the World Health Organization defined health as, **"a state of complete physical, mental and social well-being and not merely the absence of disease or infirmity."**

In this 21st Century, the integrative approach to health and healing is a blend of the best of conventional Western medicine, with the best of the "alternative" or "complementary" healing modalities. This approach to health and wellness is individualized and multidimensional, and focuses on healing and nurturing wellness from within. The integrative practitioner embraces conventional Western medical techniques, medications and treatments as well as complementary and alternative healing modalities, melding the best practices of each to provide the best care for the patient.

It is a preventive, proactive approach to health and wellness that focuses on the whole being...the totality of the individual. The patient and practitioner collaborate to create and maintain optimal health and well-being of body, mind, and spirit, and it is a dynamic and lifelong partnership. Along with Hippocrates, I believe we as human beings have the instinct and innate ability to restore balance in our whole selves and with guidance and support we can create, maintain, and sustain our own health and wellness.

The Duke Wheel of Health

This integrative approach is best illustrated by the Duke Wheel of Health, which was developed by Duke Integrative Medicine, part of the Duke University Health system.

Duke Integrative Medicine

■ Self-Care   ▨ Professional Care

The Duke Wheel of Health emphasizes and reflects the importance of the individual and his role in his own health, happiness and vitality. The individual is front and center in the Wheel of Health, mindfully paying attention to the various aspects and components of health: Movement, Exercise and Rest; Nutrition; Personal and Professional Development; Physical Environment; Relationships and Communication; Spirituality; and Mind-Body Connection. The maintenance of health and wellness requires the individual to be present and notice what is happening in each of these areas.

Through the coaching process, you discover how to pay attention, monitor, and make adjustments as needed to preserve balance and harmony in the various areas of health. As you identify and understand the impact of your lifestyle and behavior on health and wellness, you can design and own the changes needed in order to create and maintain better health. It is your vision and values, the reasons for change that provide the motivation and determination to change the behavior.

The outermost ring on the wheel consists of professional care (prevention and intervention) by integrative physicians and health professionals, utilizing conventional and complementary approaches to health and healing. The practitioners deliver, coordinate, and manage professional care, as needed by the patient.

Look at each area on the wheel yourself. In which areas are you strong? Are there other areas that are weaker? You can rate yourself in each area of the wheel on a scale of one to ten. What number best describes where you are today? What number would you like to be on this area of the wheel? What must you do to achieve this?

Client and Coach - Partners for Health

Integrative health coaching takes a multidimensional approach that considers all aspects of health and healing with a focus on balance, joy, and satisfaction with life. Within this context, changes such as establishing a personal meditation practice, taking daily vitamins, clearing the clutter out of the living room, making a habit of spending more time with your spouse, following a gluten-free diet, or developing a plan to get along better with coworkers are initiated to support your personal values and vision of health. Other changes which include: drinking more water each day, making time for rest or play, making healthier food choices, using dental floss daily, getting off "autopilot" and paying better attention, having more effective time management, taking time for oneself instead of working 24/7, making time for personal activities such as reading or volunteering, taking vacations, improving communication and challenging relationships, and creating a better work or home environment can be approached from the same integrative health perspective. What brings you joy and happiness? What does having better health really mean to you? What will you be able to do (that perhaps you cannot do now) when you are healthier or more active? Anything that interferes with, disrupts, or sidetracks your vision of optimal health is the perfect subject with which to begin coaching.

Together we will take a holistic and integrative approach to your health and your overall well-being, and design and develop an overall and personalized plan for health and happiness, and make it a reality. Working within the coaching partnership you will create strategies using your strength and experiences to remove or overcome any obstacles or barriers as you move forward toward your goal. Through exploration and brainstorming, implementation, assessment, and celebration, you will create the health and happiness you desire. Resources, support and guidance will be provided to help you to make, maintain, and sustain Positive Healthstyles.

The Coaching Process

Begin by using this exercise to help you identify and clarify your values, and honor their importance to you in making a behavior change:

Close your eyes and envision your perfect day. Take yourself through the entire day, start to finish and write down in as much detail as possible what you are doing. How are you spending your time? Who are you with? How are you earning a living? What activities do you enjoy? Then look at how your current life aligns with this vision of a perfect day. If you do not make a change what will your life be like in two years? Five years? Ten years?

But if you do make the change, what will happen? What will you be doing? What else could be possible? What does this feel like? Why do you want to make the change? What elements of this vision are the most important? What really matters to you? When the behavior change is tied to a closely held personal value, you are more strongly motivated, it is easier to embrace the change, and you are more determined to achieve your goals.

Once you have pictured your ideal life of health, happiness, and vitality, compare and contrast it with your life today. Look at the Wheel of Health and decide where you would like to focus your work. What skills have you called on in the past when you needed to make a change? Can they be used in this situation? What do you need to do to prepare to make the change? Is there any reason why

27

you should not make this change? Why should you make this change? What is the impact of making the change? Once you decide where and what change you want to make, you set the goal. When you achieve the goal, your vision of health and satisfaction becomes a reality.

Next, break the goal down into action steps called SMART steps (S = specific, M = measurable, A = action-oriented, R= realistic, T= time-specific). You decide what is a small and realistically achievable step to take. How confident and ready are you to tackle this? What might prevent you from meeting the goal? What barriers or obstacles might get in the way? We add a back-up plan, a Plan B, so that you can accomplish the goal if life throws you a curve. It is important to set yourself up for success. You set the action and the time frame. To whom will you be accountable for this action?

Lastly, we assess the action. Celebrate success/partial success? Why was it only partially successful? Incomplete successes are learning opportunities, so what did you learn? How can you modify and adjust this action step now so that it is achievable? What must you do to maintain this new behavior? This is a continuous, dynamic and fluid process, revisiting and refining the goals and action steps, readjusting them as life, desires, and goals may change.

Below are examples of how two clients I have worked with have used the coaching process to make and sustain health changes that improved their lives in meaningful ways.

Joe's Story

Joe was able to make a change in his daily routine to improve his oral and overall health. I met Joe in the dental office. He brushed his teeth twice a day, but did not use dental floss, although he had been told to do so many times in the past. Flossing did not seem important to him, and besides, he didn't have time for it. His dentist told him he had a gum infection which is the beginning of periodontal disease (disease of the gums and bones surrounding the teeth). When Joe learned that having periodontal disease increases the risk of developing heart disease, he became worried. His father and his uncle had died of heart attacks and he did not want to die of a heart attack himself. Joe had a lovely wife and two small children, and his family meant the world to him. Joe wanted to be healthy to enjoy his children and his grandchildren, and if he did not change his oral hygiene routine, he would end up dead, like his father and his uncle. He wanted to start using dental floss, but how could he develop this new habit? What did Joe do in the past when he wanted to change a habit?

Joe said he had stopped smoking a few years ago and he weaned himself off cigarettes gradually until he smoked no more. He said he could use the same strategy in developing the flossing habit. He said if he was able to stop smoking which was not easy, he was certain he could start flossing, and he was ready to start right away. We looked at Joe's typical day and determined when would be the best time for him to floss. Joe was really rushed in the morning when he brushed his teeth so he didn't think he could floss then. Before bed was not a good time as he was usually so tired, he barely had energy to brush his teeth. Joe thought about other times of day, and decided he would floss when he got home from work and changed his clothes. He would make it part of his transition from his work life to his home life. He chose a back-up plan. If he did not floss when he got home from work; he would do it right after dinner. He said he would be accountable to his wife for this behavior change because she loves him and does not want him to have a heart attack. Two weeks later, Joe was happy to tell me he had flossed his teeth every day, and his mouth felt cleaner and his wife noticed his breath was fresher. Joe said there were a few days when he did not floss when he got home from work, but he did it right after dinner. His back-up plan helped him meet his goal. Most importantly, Joe said, he felt good knowing he had taken steps to avoid heart disease and possibly a premature death, and by taking better care of himself, he would be there for his family, enjoying them for many years.

Suzanne's Story

Suzanne loved to run outside after work. She ran through the parks in her neighborhood and loved the peace and freedom of running for as long as she wanted. Then autumn came and the days got shorter, it got colder, and the last thing she wanted to do was spend more time outside in the dark and the cold. When she got home from work she just wanted to snuggle under a quilt in her drafty apartment. Suzanne was torn because she loved the way she felt after a good run, and she felt she was letting herself down. Running wasn't just good exercise, it was something she did for herself.

When Suzanne looked at her daily routine and where and how she could get back to running, she came up with a plan. She decided she would wear her running clothes to bed, instead of pajamas, and as soon as she woke up in the morning, she would put on her coat and go directly to the local gym to use the treadmill and the elliptical machines. It would not be the same as running outside, but she had a video of the National Parks that she would watch as she ran in the gym. She would pack her toiletries and work clothes the night before, and have the bag packed to take to the gym. After working out, she would shower, dress, and go to work directly from there. She would implement this new plan five days a week during her work days, and her back up plan would be to go to the gym on the weekend if she were to miss a weekday. Suzanne said her roommate would hold her accountable for sticking with this. Her roommate belonged to the same gym, and often accompanied her. Suzanne was happy that she had found a way to continue running in the cold weather. An added bonus was that Suzanne and her roommate had a better relationship now that they were working out together.

Both Joe and Suzanne successfully made changes in their be-havior, which supported, enriched, and reinforced their values and vision of better overall health and happiness. By partnering with their coach, Joe and Suzanne were able to determine what change to make and how to implement it. Their coach helped them identify inner strengths and strategies that they had used successfully in the past, and that they could employ once again to make this change. The mo-tivation and determination for change came from within; the coach was a guide and facilitator in the change process.

You have all you need inside of you to make changes in your life. You know what is important to you and what makes you happy. You can visualize your life with this change, and all the possibilities and opportunities this could create. Working with the coach to explore, brainstorm, set a plan of action and implement it will create the Positive Healthstyles to attain the life of happiness and satisfaction you deserve.

Christel Autuori believes in a multidimensional, holistic, interactive, and preventive approach to health and vitality, and is passionate about helping people create, maintain, and sustain optimal health and happiness. She is the founder and owner of Integrative Health of Connecticut, providing integrative health coaching and holistic stress management services as well as yoga instruction and workshops to individuals, groups, and organizations. She is a professional speaker, author, educator, consultant, and practitioner. Christel is a partner and guide for her clients as they paint a picture of optimal health and what it means to them and for their life. Together they explore and examine areas of imbalance and dis-ease, and create and implement a realistic, practical, personalized plan for change— Positive HealthStyles—with a holistic approach to health and happiness in life. Christel is a registered dental hygienist, registered yoga teacher, certified Reiki master, certified holistic stress management instructor, and a certified integrative health coach. She has a Masters' degree in Integrative Health and Healing and is a graduate of the Integrative Health Coach Professional Training program at Duke Integrative Medicine. She is a founder of the Global Integrative Health Coaching Alliance (www.gihca.org) and an adjunct faculty member at Western Connecticut State University. Christel Autuori, RDH, RYT, MA, CICH, 203.788.0647, www.integrativehealthct.com.

Chapter 4

Living Authentically

Christine Bilotti Peterson, MBA

What does living authentically really mean? When you are living authentically, you are living the way you want to live. You are living the best version of yourself. You are satisfying the areas in your life that are important to you. A critical component in transforming your life to being more authentic is being very intentional about your time. Here are some of the things I hear from clients with whom I begin coaching assignments:

- *What can I do to get more balance in my life? I'm running around doing all these things but I'm not happy. I feel like I've been sleepwalking through life.*
- *Can you help me figure out what I really want to do?*
- *I'm in a job that I'm not inspired by, where do I go next?*

There are several steps to helping someone build an authentic and intentional life, and I will outline some helpful steps to take you on this journey. How can you accomplish the goals you set, how to take time for yourself, and how to spend the time on exactly what it takes to accomplish your priorities and goals? All of these things are the ingredients to build a recipe adding up to living authentically where you specifically plan the way you want to live, and you maximize your time to achieve your goals.

Step one is authenticity inside of you: being true to yourself, serving what you think and feel, trusting in your beliefs, values, morals and goals. Step two is authenticity externally: being true to others, having what you say and do follow from what you think and feel. As you ascend in your journey to authenticity, the more authentic you are to yourself; your happiness follows and then flows to others.

Lever One-Assess Where You Are

The first step in the transformation to authenticity is truly asking yourself where you are now, and how you feel about it. How has the last year been for you? Where do you feel accomplished? Where do you need to spend more time and effort? What do you REALLY want?

In the wheel of life, there are essentially eight categories to assess. There are two aspects of rating these categories. The first is: how important is this category at this point in your life? (One being a low level of importance or not very important at this time; ten being extremely important at this time in your life.) The second rating is what level have you achieved, (one being a low level of achievement thus far; 10 being the highest level, a level that meets your authentic inner level of satisfaction).

1) Career - Importance rating: _____ Level achieved: _____

2) Family and Friends-Importance rating:_____ Level achieved: _____

3) Significant Other-Importance rating: _____ Level achieved: _____

4) Fun-Importance rating: _____ Level achieved: _____

5) Health/Wellness-Importance rating: _____ Level achieved: _____

6) Finances-Importance rating: _____ Level achieved: _____

7) Personal Growth-Importance rating: _____ Level achieved: _____

8) Home/Organization-Importance rating: _____ Level achieved: _____

Once you have rated these and truly thought through the different aspects of each topic, your next step is to choose the top three areas you would like to focus on for the next year. These areas may likely be your lowest ratings, or maybe not. Maybe you rated yourself middle of the road, but really want to take this priority to the next level. At different points in your life, different things matter most and rise to the top. It is almost impossible for someone to be a 10 in all categories at all times. As someone entering a new stretch position in their career, that may be the focus area of that time. As a new Mom, family may be the most important area that year. If you have just had a health scare or are not feeling well, wellness might be the focus for you. Living authentically means this is not what someone else thinks you should do---this is about YOU. What do YOU really want? What do YOU need? What is going to make YOU happy? What serves YOU? Some categories may be fine at a 5, where other categories may be so important, anything less than a 9 doesn't work for you.

Lever Two-Goal Setting

Now that you've selected your top 3 priority areas, it is time to create that future vision. Setting a vision is an important part of the journey. Think BIG. Remember that a vision doesn't have boundaries. Imagine yourself in the future at your ultimate... state your greatest wishes and dreams. If you can have anything what would it be? When you envision your future state in this category, what will this look like? What will you be doing? How will you feel? What is different? Let me use Health and Wellness as a focus area.

My vision: In this area I am imagining myself the picture of health. I am strong and lean. My face looks refreshed and I am smiling. I look happy, relaxed, and even younger. There is a sparkle in my eye. My clothes fit well. I have incredible energy. I am cooking healthy organic food and enjoy sharing these meals with my family. This is my future.

Now that you have your vision and you can actually see yourself in this future state, you now need to create a simply stated goal for the year to help you attain that future vision. Be as specific as you can. Here is an example:

My goal: To become healthier, lose 20 pounds, work out daily and eat more nutritious foods.

Do you know it is a proven fact that people who write down their goals are ten times more likely to achieve them? So many people are running through life so fast that they don't stop and take the time to assess where they are and decide what exactly it is that they want. In fact many times during my coaching sessions, half of the work is figuring out what a person is striving for and what is going to make them happy. The second half is putting plans together on achieving those goals in a particular timeframe.

Lever Three-Action Planning

Once your main goal is known action steps must be created to bring this goal to life. Action planning can be fun. Experimentation and continuing to pursue different strategies helps goals to be achieved. On the other hand, if you find a consistent way of attaining a goal, it may work for you to keep repeating that. Everyone is unique, find what works for you.

Annual goal action planning happens in three timelines: daily/ weekly; monthly; and quarterly. (If you have a goal that requires a shorter timeline or longer timeline, an action plan timeline might be different for you.) Secondly, and just as critical, will be to celebrate your successes, no matter how small.

Take each one of your priorities and begin your action planning. In continuing with the health and wellness example:

Daily/Weekly:
What will I do daily or weekly to move me toward my goal?
E.g.: work out for 30 min a day _____.

Monthly:
What will I do monthly to move me toward my goal?
E.g: Pinterest and prepare new healthy recipes _____.
How will I celebrate successes?
E.g: I will treat myself to a manicure _____.

Quarterly:
What will I do quarterly to move me toward my goal?
E.g: Try a new exercise class _____.
How will I celebrate successes?
E.g: I will treat myself to a new workout outfit _____.

Lever Four-Celebrating Successes

Celebrating your successes and incenting yourself to continue on this journey to transformation is critical to the process. The perspectives you have on your goals is a key reason of whether people keep going and reach their goals, or begin to avoid or resent them. Perspective is about choice and it is a powerful tool. You have the choice to look at things through an optimistic lens or a pessimistic lens.

For example, regarding health and wellness: I had a client who began every morning by negatively reflecting on all the things she did not like about herself when she looked in the mirror. The goal of losing weight came from a very negative perspective. We worked on changing her perspective and looking at the positive. We shifted the goal from losing weight to getting healthy and having more energy. We added components to her plan like experimenting with new healthy food. We also added items like trying fun and different exercise classes like Zumba, Barre Pilates and Spinning, rather than running which she began to despise and was painful for her body. She began having so much fun with this goal that she focused less and less on what the scale said and more on having fun experimenting with her plan. Eventually the scale started moving farther and farther downward. It changed the way she was looking at all of her focus areas. She redid her plan for all and made sure the plan and goal was focused with a positive orientation. Needless to say she achieved her goals and is now leading a happier and more authentic life.

Throughout this journey you will have peaks and valleys. You will learn what inspires you. You will assess and reflect after a pitfall. You will discover what triggers throw you off course. It is helpful to talk about these things, whether it is with a coach, a trainer or a friend. This leads to our next lever.

Lever Five-Accountability and Support

The next lever to pull to help you reach your goals is taking the step of accountability and support. No one needs to go it alone. There are people all around you to help you through this transformation. I have never in my life personally or with a client, had someone ask for help and not receive it. It is actually a beautiful thing. It is important that you think of this before your journey begins. Some questions to ask: Who in my life will I ask for help with this goal? What resources can I use to support me through this journey? Is there a program I can join to help me? Who might be a mentor or sponsor for me? Do I know anyone with a similar goal? How can I ask my family to support me? Writing down names and contact information and reaching out to them along the way is an essential step in the journey. Ask for help, ask for feedback, and ask for support. Call these people on tough days. You do not need to go this alone.

Accountability and Support System:

Coach: _____ Resources: _____
Programs: _____ Mentors: _____
Online Tools: _____ Friends/Family: _____

What happens if you go off track? Sometimes when people stumble during their journey, they take this as an excuse to throw in the towel and give up. This does not have to be the case. In fact, you will stumble…plan on it, as this is very natural. The most important thing to do is have the strength to get back on the plan. Reset yourself. Start fresh. It may be psychologically easiest for you to start at the next first of the month or the next Monday. Sometimes a break for thinking and doing is the restart needed to take your actions, goals and commitment to the next level. Most importantly, it is ok. Plan to take a break.

A very important trait that most people need to continually work on their entire lives is Grit. This trait is not only one of life-long learning, but it is a differentiating trait for success in all of us. Grit plays out on the kindergarten playground to the sports field, from the hospital room to the board room. The term Grit used psychologically is the 'non cognitive trait that involves perseverance of effort to accomplish a long-term goal no matter what obstacles or challenges lay within a 'gritty' individual's path.' Essentially what research is telling us is that no matter how smart someone is, or how good they are at an activity or game, it essentially doesn't matter if they don't combine that skill with Grit.

Top five key attributes to having high grit:

a. A clear goal, purpose and vision
b. Determination and inner strength irrelevant of other's doubts
c. Self-confidence to figure it out
d. Humbleness about knowing it doesn't come easy
e. Patience and flexibility for the small stuff that gets in the way

Here is a quiz to see how much Grit you have. This will be a good test for you to take quarterly and decide how you can keep evolving through this process to increase your grit factor.

The Grit Quiz: How Gritty are you? What's your Grit #?
Score yourself from 1-5; 1=never, 2=rarely, 3=sometimes, 4=often, 5=always

1. I overcome setbacks to conquer challenges. _____
2. New ideas and projects do not distract me from previous ones. _____
3. My interests change from year to year. _____
4. I am not discouraged by setbacks. _____
5. I am a hard worker. _____
6. I have no difficulty maintaining focus. _____
7. I have achieved a goal that took years of work. _____

Scoring:
26 or higher = Strong Grit score-you have the ability for long-term persistence, courage and strength.
16-25 = Solid Grit score-you normally persist through difficult times; occasionally it may take extra time and strength to continue.
Below 15 = Low Grit-Focus on developing this muscle and capability.

Lever Six: Organization and Time Management

Being prepared, organized and taking control of your calendar is an essential step in reaching your goals. I normally suggest people start with scheduling a week ahead, tactically, holding sections of your calendar each day to focus on each action item. Some goals may require a one hour a week hold; others may be a daily 30 minutes. Scheduling this time, helps you maintain the consistency needed for achievement. Letting your calendar happen to you, is when things will fall apart. Setting up this cadence from the start will help you avoid pitfalls.

Monthly, a successful strategy for my clients has been to utilize the Look Forward/Look Back tool. This is a tool used to continue to hone in on mastering your organization and time management. It helps you figure out what is monopolizing your time and resets the opportunity to make you even more intentional and focused for the next month. This tool can be used in multiple situations and even in professional environments to master your skills and maximize your time.

 Look Forward/Look Back Tool

Review your calendar for the last month. Develop a picture of how you spent your time. Ask yourself: was that the right time allocation? What should I change? What worked? How can I replicate it next month?

Look at the next month. Ask yourself what are my top 3 priorities? What do I need to do to maximize my next month? What are key actions I can plan for? Is my schedule set up to best achieve my goals?

In conclusion, I'm excited for you to reflect, assess, set goals and plan to achieve them. There is no reason to let another day pass without you focused on creating the life you truly, authentically want to live. Bring out the best in yourself, and enjoy every day doing it!

Christine Bilotti Peterson has over 20 years of experience in the financial services industry where she has held a variety of Human Resource leadership positions. Christine earned her undergraduate degree in Marketing and Communications at Central Connecticut State University and completed her MBA at The Lally School of Business at Rensselear Polytechnic University. Christine became a Certified Executive Coach in 2013 through the International Coaching Federation. She passionately enjoys working with clients to create their aspirational goals and achieve them both personally and professionally. For more information or assistance to help you reach your goals, live life more authentically, and create the life you want to live, please contact, Executive Coach: Christine Bilotti Peterson at cbpeterson@me.com.

Chapter 5

Stay Conscious in Your Relationships
Stop the Addiction to Drama

Diane Hayden, PhD

My motto for a long time has been; do not create drama and do not feed into it. Many of my clients have asked me, "What do you mean by drama?" I think we all may have different definitions, but for me drama can be defined as: a way of relating to the world in which a person consistently overreacts to or greatly exaggerates the importance of benign events. I often find that typically drama is used by people who are chronically bored or those who seek attention.

Here are some common signs of drama:

1. Having one supposedly serious problem after another.

2. Constantly telling other people about one's problems.

3. Having extreme or frequently shifting, intense emotions on a seemingly daily basis.

4. Claiming to have experienced negative events that are questionable.

5. A pattern of irrational behavior and reactions to everyday problems.

Yet why are we so addicted to it? Why do we put ourselves in positions that we know will add drama to our lives? Is it the instant gratification of a situation that feels really good at the time, even though we know it will cause pain and suffering to ourselves and others in the long run? Is it always a conscious decision or do we make choices based on some subconscious message? Is it easier to live with drama than to create a life without it?

No matter what the answers to these questions are, the bottom line is that more often than not you know when you're creating drama and sometimes you still do it. You also know when the important people in your life are creating drama.

**The challenge is to commit to eliminating the drama...
being aware of when you're creating it and choosing to stop,
and making the decision to walk away from people in
your life that are unwilling to stop.**

Watch Those Powerful Thoughts

As I think about all the times in my life when I've either created drama or allowed myself to become entangled in someone else's drama, I have to wonder...what was I thinking? Or maybe the better question is – was I thinking at all? And that to me is the heart of the matter.

**Drama can only occur when you're not paying close
attention to what kinds of thoughts you're entertaining.**

Typically...the negative ones. It can only happen when the ego is in charge and you haven't taken the time to step back and be the observer. Because once you do that and analyze your thoughts and actions from an objective perspective, you can't help but realize that engaging in drama is really a no-win situation.

Sometimes we do not even realize that we are spending most of our time in negative thought processes because we are so used to saying the same things to ourselves over and over. We get used to hearing the same negative self-talk and it becomes our normal state. But if we check in with how we're feeling (happy, joyful, excited vs. sad, angry or depressed) we know immediately whether we're in a positive or negative thought process.

How do you feel when you engage in drama with a friend or family member? Do those feelings make you feel good about yourself or not?

Usually if you're not feeling good, then that's the first step in becoming aware that you might be engaging in drama.

Here's a typical train of thought for most of us…"I wonder if he's thinking about me (in reference to a spouse, significant other or potential new love interest), why hasn't he called yet, why is it so late and he isn't home yet, I wonder if he's cheating on me, …" Are you exhausted yet? Thinking, thinking, thinking and where does it get us?

We all let our thoughts and emotions get carried away sometimes, it's human nature. But when it gets to the point that all you're doing is working yourself into a frenzy because of some potential negative outcome that may not even happen, that's creating drama and that's where you need to draw the line. That's when you need to take a step back, listen to the voice in your head objectively and become the observer. We're all going to have negative thoughts, and it's next to impossible to stop them when they come, but the difference between becoming consumed with them or stepping outside the ego into a peaceful place is what will allow us to live our lives free from drama.

It's a conscious choice that you can decide to make.

Drama in Relationships

While I believe we can create drama in any area of our lives, I find more often than not, that typically most of us create drama in our relationships. The opportunities are endless. In fact, over the last month I've seen the following: a friend who is going through an ugly divorce, another friend who calls me daily to get advice about dating, and two friends who are butting heads and calling me to talk about the other one and then posting random comments on Facebook to irritate each other. You can take any of these situations and see how one can get totally caught up in the drama if you don't make a continuous effort to watch your thoughts.

Let's take the situation with my friend and the dating advice because you don't see much more drama than what goes on in the dating scene. I find that most people either love dating or they hate it and just want to hurry up and find someone they're compatible with so they can avoid the whole process. I happen to think it's fascinating and the stories I hear never cease to amaze me about how people interact and treat each other as they're just beginning to get to know one another.

So, this friend of mine is dating a man that she's really interested in. He's appearing to be a tricky one. One week hot and heavy with her, the next week it seems she's out of sight, out of mind. Of course this allows for a never ending stream of phone calls to me with the topic of discussion typically being – you guessed it, what he's thinking/feeling/doing. Here we go with the drama…in my friend's own words, "do you think there's someone else, why doesn't he want to spend more time with me, how come he appears to be so interested one minute and not the next, maybe he has a girlfriend, is he just not that into me?" and on and on. Now I could easily feed into her drama and spend hours on the phone analyzing his behavior of the week and I have to admit…sometimes I do. But most of the time I'm trying to get her to disengage from this thought process and spend more time focusing on herself and what she wants instead of worrying about him.

Drama has a way of sneaking up on you, causing your head to spin with all kinds of negative thoughts and before you know it, you've spent hours creating imaginary situations in your head of the worst possible outcome.

In her mind, she's been getting dumped by this guy every other week for the last two months in a myriad of awful scenarios. We just had a conversation today because this is one of those weeks where he's disappeared and she's freaking out that he's decided it's over. I told her that she had two choices, she could either choose to live in fear, worry and anxiety about what's going to happen next, or she could choose to be peaceful and happy and hold the space for him to come to her. If he has decided he doesn't want to see her again, then there will be plenty of time then to cry and feel pain. Why put yourself through it now, when you don't even know what the outcome is yet. She spends so much time wondering what he's thinking and whether or not he likes her, that she doesn't even give herself the opportunity to really evaluate what he can offer her and if SHE is truly into him.

Focus on Yourself First

Why not focus on yourself and figure out what you want? You see, in order to do that, you need to manage your thoughts and that's where the hard work comes in. As I am constantly telling my friend, you need to make time during the day for meditation and quieting the mind. It works every time – even when I resist it. Every time those negative, anxious, worrisome thoughts come into your head, you need to quiet them.

If you don't have time to sit in your meditation chair, then you need to find a flip switch – something you can think about that will make you happy and joyful – and you need to employ that switch the minute you start to head down the path of negative thinking.

This is the only way you'll ever get out. It seems so easy and yet sometimes it's so hard to do.

What I've realized as I've studied this more and more is that there are certain people who have amazing, joyful, and successful lives and others who seem to be constantly enmeshed in drama, pain and anxiety. The difference between these two groups of people is that the former are able to use their thoughts to help them create what they want in their lives and eliminate or pay less attention to the thoughts that cause them grief or anxiety, while the latter tend to focus only on the thoughts that keep them in the midst of the drama.

The only question for you is… which group do you want to be in?

Research has shown that strong emotions can actually cause positive and negative biochemical changes in the body. If you are cut off from your emotions or feelings, they will eventually manifest as a physical symptom or disease. We all know that stress is the number one cause of many chronic diseases, but what is stress a result of…either suppressing your emotions completely or spending most of the time focusing on negative emotions. Until we can express, feel and appreciate our emotions, they will block our energy and we will be unable to live in a healthy state at our fullest capacity. Once we understand that we can control our emotions by monitoring our thoughts and staying in the present moment, then we can fulfill our true destiny.

Easier said than done… probably so! However, we can definitely master this game with conscious effort over time. The first step is to appreciate that your experience in life has nothing to do with the external events that happen to you.

In other words, nothing in life has any meaning unless you give meaning to it.

That's why the same event can happen to two different people and they may each have a drastically different response to it. If you watch people driving in rush hour traffic, you'll see this example played out on a daily basis…some people remain totally calm and others go into a terrific road rage.

Your feelings affect your results in life because you first have a thought about something, then you create an emotion around that thought and then feelings come into your body to merge the thought and emotion. Before you know it you are caught up in a vicious cycle of thought – emotion – feeling – thought – emotion – feeling, and usually it's a negative cycle. You have to be able to recognize the feelings you're having and interrupt the cycle. Feelings of doubt, insecurity, fear, and anger are all biofeedback mechanisms notifying you that you are in an unhealthy pattern and work needs to be done to get out. Every time you have these feelings, ask yourself these questions.

"What does this emotional reaction say about me?"
"What do I have to believe to be
experiencing this emotion right now?"

Those answers will be a great insight into changing your belief system about the kinds of experiences you have and thus the kind of life you live.

You truly choose your path in this life, but you must make a decision to be disciplined and determined about monitoring your thoughts and emotions. Most people are unwilling to pay this price as it is work that must be consistently done on a daily basis. Emotion is energy in motion; it's up to you in what direction it moves.

Leaving the Drama Behind

It's hard enough eliminating your own focus on drama, but what do you do when you're surrounded by people in your life that constantly engage in drama?

How do you leave behind people that you've been friends with for years but all they want to do is gossip and bring you down?

How do you leave a relationship with someone that you may be physically attracted to, but who constantly pushes your buttons and is unwilling to work on creating a conscious, peaceful relationship?

How do you deal with a parent that gives you guilt trips and drags you into family arguments?

All of these are very valid situations and tough decisions to make if you really want to eliminate all of the drama from your life. And, sometimes if you don't make the move yourself, you'll get a little kick in the butt from the Universe!

First, as you begin to become more aware of when you're causing drama and disengage from that, you'll begin to see your other relationships in a much clearer light. Seeing your friend or significant other in a situation where you question their integrity just might be the incentive you need to move on from that relationship. You can always surround yourself with new friends and find a new love relationship. Easier said than done, you say? I do realize that for many people this can be very difficult and overwhelming. Maybe the last thing you want to do is get back into the dating world. But I would ask you to think about how staying in a bad relationship will ultimately affect you emotionally and physiologically. Many times when I've struggled to leave a relationship I've thought to myself – it would be better to be alone than to be in a toxic relationship.

Removing yourself from drama in a family situation is a little more difficult as most people probably don't want to cut ties to their parents or siblings, however, in some extreme cases, I have known people to do that. In this case, you really only have a couple of options. You can have a serious discussion with your family member and let them know that you won't tolerate the behavior any longer and explain why. Hopefully, they will understand and agree to eliminate drama as well. Or if they are unwilling to stop, then you may need to limit the amount of time you spend with them.

Secondly, leaving behind things that no longer serve you allow you to maintain and raise your level of positive energy or vibration. Everything is made of energy and energy is all around us and moving through us. Energy from humans comes from highly charged emotions to create electromagnetic wave patterns of energy. These vibrations or energies filter out into the universe and look to attach to something or someone with a similar vibration and eventually bring that outcome back to the original person. If you allow yourself to stay in unhealthy relationships or to be attracted to people that continually hurt you, you will attract more negative occurrences and you will continue to attract this until you change your emotion or vibration. This is why it is so important that we maintain a healthy energy flow throughout our body and mind.

Even though many of these situations can be extremely painful and leave you feeling hurt, rejected or emotionally drained, I do believe that they happen for a reason and that reason is to allow you to move on to a better place. It opens up the space in your life for you to find the people who are your true friends and soulmates, the people who are vibrating at the same level that you are and who will help you continue to grow and develop instead of holding you back. And it's the Universe's way of giving us that little nudge we all need sometimes to keep us moving and growing on our path of personal and spiritual development. And for that we should be grateful. So, the next time you see someone's true colors and it's not a beautiful rainbow, just say thank you and keep on moving! Life is too short to be addicted to drama.

Dr. Diane Hayden is the owner and publisher of Natural Nutmeg Magazine, Essential Living Maine Magazine and Nutmeg Creative Media. She is a speaker, writer and workshop facilitator. She holds a B.S. in Marketing from the University of Connecticut, a Ph.D. in Exercise Physiology from the University of Maryland and is an Empowerment Life Coach. For 20 years, her work has focused on inspiring individuals to learn about the power of thought and emotion and how it shapes their lives. Her passion centers on helping even just one person navigate the dating scene and find the perfect partner with whom they can share their life. You can learn more about her online at http:naturalnutmeg.com/category/where-is-dr-di-travel or http:drdianehayden.com.

Chapter 6

Coaching Baby Boomer Couples
Creating Vibrant and Fulfilling
Lives in Partnership

Andrew L. Miser, PhD, CPCC, PCC

Baby boomers are the cohort of people born after World War II between 1946 and 1964 and who came of age during a time when American society was undergoing great transformative change. If you are a baby boomer, you witnessed the civil rights movement and the Vietnam protests of the 1960s, the women's rights movement and the sexual revolution of the 1970s and the advent of the human potential movement. You also experienced the beginning of a decades long slowing of income growth, which required many baby boomer couples to become dual income earners to be able to buy a home and support a family.

The social fabric between men and women has changed dramatically during your lifetime. The defined marital roles of the 1950s became a thing of the past. Husbands and wives began forging a new kind of marriage based in love, choice, equality, fairness and personal growth. The trend toward both individuals focusing on their careers, self-development and happiness put new pressures on the institution of marriage. During this time, if you weren't happy in your marriage, you could more easily get a divorce. In coming years, you and your cohort as a whole are likely to live longer than previous generations, which will create new marital challenges as you advance into your senior years.

In the 1970s and 80s, you had a number of resources to support you in your marital success and happiness. Marriage and family therapy had become a well-established mental health profession. Marital education and marriage encounter groups were becoming increasingly available. There were also many weekend self-empowerment groups, which promised personal effectiveness and fulfillment. And, finally, bookstores exploded with self-help books on topics, ranging from relationship advice and healthy eating to twelve-step support and managing one's time effectively.

Baby Boomers Today

Today, the youngest baby boomers have turned 50 years old; the oldest are closing in on age 70. Baby boomers are experiencing many life transitions, including their adult children going to college, getting married and starting a family; the aging and death of their parents; changes in their careers; new health concerns and downsizing at home. The divorce rate among baby boomers is currently higher than the divorce rates for every other generation and this increase in divorce is occurring when the divorce rate for married couples generally is actually declining, if only slightly! Some of the possible reasons for this trend are:

- While raising their children and building their careers, baby boomer couples failed to invest in the health and well-being of their relationship.
- Couples today are confronting the reality of their lives and the unhappy state of their marriages as their grown children are leaving home.
- Many baby boomer women have had professional careers, which allow them greater choice to live independently.

With your children leaving home and your careers almost complete, you like other baby boomer couples may be looking for a new purpose for your individual lives and in your marriage. You want your lives to be creative, fulfilling and contributing on your own terms.

The Value of Coaching for Baby Boomer Couples

If you are a baby boomer couple, a coaching relationship can be of significant value in helping you to design a fulfilling life together. In such a relationship, you can put your attention squarely on the quality of your marriage and the life you both want to build. A professional coach, trained in working with couples, can assist you in having the conversations that are necessary to clarify your interests and your passions, explore new avenues of contribution, and work in partnership with each other to achieve new dreams.

1. Focusing on the Quality of Your Partnership

At this stage of your lives, you and your spouse may feel as though you are living parallel lives and yearn to reconnect with each other. This is a crucial time for you to reinvest in your marriage and to put your focus on the quality of your partnership. It is important that you reclaim time for your marriage, nurture your friendship, renew your passion and create romance. You may want to explore how to bring play and fun into your relationship by planning special dates, weekend getaways and great vacations.

A coach will support you in being in alignment around what matters most to you both and what quality of life the two of you wish to create. For instance, what are you committed to at this stage in your lives? What is important for you in terms of the well-being of your relationship? What kind of social life do you want to have and how do you wish to express yourselves with your friends? What kinds of meaningful activities (recreational, cultural, civic, etc.) do you want to plan? Working together to create a collage of pictures that capture your desired quality of life is an excellent way for you and your partner to share a vision of your partnership.

In your shared life there are many areas that require connection, teamwork and partnership. These include home care, finances, parenting, play and planning for the future. A coach can assist you in discerning where in your life together you want a greater sense of partnership and in determining what obstacles may be in the way of creating a better working relationship in your marriage. Creating a sense of partnership in areas where it has been absent for some time can bring a renewed sense of possibility as you both consider the future you wish to build.

If you are experiencing changes and transitions in family life, being able to maintain a sense of balance and perspective can make all the difference. A coach can work with you to examine where you feel out of balance, where you feel you have little choice and where you may have disempowering perspectives about the events that are occurring in your lives. Examining the impact of such points of view on the quality of your marriage and working together to create new perspectives will give you both a greater sense of freedom, power and balance in the face of challenging circumstances.

2. Adjusting to the Changing Roles with Aging Parents and Adult Children

Two of the most important challenges for baby boomers today are supporting their children as they leave home to go to college, work or enter the armed forces and helping their own parents manage their medical and financial concerns. It is an important time to reassess your roles and responsibilities with your parents and with your adult children. What is your commitment to your aging parents? What do you want for your adult children? What are your expectations, joys and fears related to the transitions they are now experiencing?

A coach can help you to frame your conversations in productive ways, adopt empowering perspectives when discussing family commitments and take action to create the kind of relationships that will support everyone in your family. What are you looking forward to in your relationship with your aging parents and adult children? What do you appreciate about the accomplishments of your adult children? What are you grateful for in your relationship with your parents? What do you and your spouse want to be acknowledged for?

3. Letting Go of Disappointments and Looking to the Future

After raising a family and investing in careers over your lifetime, you and your spouse, if you are like many other baby boomer couples today, may be experiencing uncertainty as you look to your future. This is an important time for you to evaluate the current status of your lives, assess at what crossroads you find yourselves and begin to examine what kind of life you wish to design moving forward.

Acknowledging and accepting what you have or haven't accomplished provides a powerful platform for creating what is next in your lives. What is completing and coming to a close? What are you proud of or pleased with? What regrets are you willing to give up? What disappointments and failures do you want to let go of? What new opportunities are opening up? What new challenges are you facing as a couple? What new dreams are you both excited about?

You each may find that there are significant hurts and issues that remain unresolved in your marriage. With your coach, you and your spouse will be supported in communicating effectively by making your needs and wants known to each other, by listening to each other compassionately and by making requests and promises of each other that resolves issues in your marriage to your mutual satisfaction. While not equipped to take on difficult mental health issues, a coach can assist you and your spouse in finding a marriage and family therapist or other kinds of professional help if an issue becomes an impediment to moving forward in your lives.

4. Creating a Vision of the Future

Standing in a vision of the quality of life you want to create together, you can dream new dreams, explore a new purpose for your lives and create a vision for your future. A coach is someone who will stand with you, champion your greatness and encourage you both to let go of limiting beliefs about what you think is possible. A coach may challenge you to explore activities and adventures you've never considered before. What are your fears and what stops you from taking risks? What are your deepest desires? What inspires you? What do you feel called to do? What new purpose(s) is bubbling up inside of you? A coach will assist you both to draw on your inner resources and have the difficult conversations in charting a new direction for your lives.

When envisioning a new future together, you and your partner can share with each other what you each desire in such areas as your home, family, friends, community, work, retirement, recreation and health. A coach will encourage you to step into those future images and experience what it is like having that future be real. Where are you living? What do you experience? What does it look like? What is it that lights you both up about what you envision? You can look from the future to the present time, which allows you to see, sense and feel your future in a very tangible way.

Envisioning the future together is one accomplishment; committing to that future in partnership is another important conversation to have with each other. Buying a new home, moving, creating a new business, investing money and planning for retirement are all examples of important life choices. You and your spouse can use a coach to help clarify a choice you are considering, discuss the pros and cons of that choice and make your commitment freely and powerfully in partnership. This kind of commitment is transformational in nature as it is the first major step in bringing forth the future you both envision.

5. Taking Action to Fulfill your Vision

As soon as you make a commitment to create a new future together, action plans and projects will require your immediate attention. Creating projects that are time-limited with specific intended results is an excellent way to work together as partners in areas of your life, such as home improvement plans, family get-togethers, new business ventures or ideas for a great vacation. Fulfilling projects require teamwork around planning, taking committed action and being responsible for the results of those actions, both intended and unintended.

A coach will encourage your teamwork and hold you both accountable around taking the action you deem necessary to complete your projects and fulfill the future you've envisioned. Being in alignment around the future you are creating and being held to account for taking action to fulfill your future allows you both to experience yourselves as partners on the same court of life, co-creating your lives together.

Lastly, a coach will support you and your partner to share what you enjoy about your life together. You are encouraged to share what you appreciate about each other, what strengths and talents you see in each other and what you are thankful for in your relationship. Appreciation is a powerful antidote to taking each other for granted. Appreciation helps to reveal the beauty and durability of your relationship.

Summary

At this time in your lives when your children are leaving home and your careers may be winding down, it is time for you to create your lives on your terms. This is the time for you to build a future and a life together that is creative, engaging, and fulfilling. You want to dream big, take risks and design a new purpose for your lives. You want the quality of your partnership and your marriage to be active and vibrant. In a relationship with a professional coach, you have a powerful resource you can draw on to re-invent your lives, find new ways to contribute, design an exciting future and work together to create and enjoy a life you love.

Andrew Miser is a professional coach who specializes in coaching baby boomer couples in designing a shared life of passion, fulfillment and contribution. Andy recently published a book entitled The Partnership Marriage: Creating the Life You Love...Together. Working with couples individually and in groups, he supports couples in clarifying what's important to them, creating a shared vision of the future and taking action to fulfill the future they've envisioned. Andy has developed an innovative coaching curriculum designed for couples committed to bringing greater partnership into their lives. Prior to focusing exclusively on partnership marriage, Andy was a psychologist and marriage and family therapist in private practice in Hartford, Connecticut. He has a Ph.D. in Developmental Psychology from The University of Connecticut. Andy was trained as a Co-active Coach through the Coaches Training Institute (CTI) and is currently on the faculty of CTI. Andy is a member of the American Psychological Association, a Clinical Member of the American Association of Marriage and Family Therapy and a Professional Certified Coach with the International Coach Federation. Andy lives in Boston with his wife and partner, Martha. They've been married for 40 years. Andrew L. Miser, Ph.D., CPCC, PCC, 617-942-2757, andy@ thepartnershipmarriage.com.

Chapter 7

Accelerate the Growth of Your Business and Career with Your Money Mindset

Creating a Money Mindset for Women Entrepreneurs and Professional Women to Have Courageous Money Conversations, Boldly Stand in Their Value and Master Their Cash Flow

Mamak Charepoo, MM, MFA,
Advanced Trainer NHA®,SMA®

Five months before I started my Money Mindset coaching business, I found myself in a very frustrated position. I had only one client in my parenting coaching business that year and I was fed up with running my "passion" and not having a business.

I looked hard at myself and thought, "How come such an intelligent, talented and creative person cannot figure out the "money thing" in her business?"

My life flashed before me.

With two master's degrees in music, for 15 years I had enjoyed working with singers, flautists and cellists as a collaborative pianist in bringing out the best in their performance. As an artist I loved what I was doing and did not pay too much attention to the money aspect of having a freelance career.

After I divorced and became the sole provider for my children I was scared to death. How was I going to support my family? I had not built my passion for working with other musicians as a career that could support a family. After begging God for help, I was offered a very rewarding job for a limited time in empowering neighborhood volunteers to teach spiritual classes to children in their neighborhood. Once again I loved what I was doing but did not use the temporary position as a stepping stone for the next success in my life.

I remarried and started a parenting coaching company with a friend. After the first year of depleting our connections with school administrators, parents and teachers, we had to actually market ourselves! That meant talking about our fees, the value we gave to others and promoting ourselves. I had one client that whole year!

I started seeing a pattern. I would do an excellent job, get referrals for more opportunities and somewhere along the line I would sabotage myself. It was not from lack of opportunities that I had never developed a thriving business, but it was my mindset around money that governed the decisions I made that ultimately undermined and sabotaged my successes.

At that point of frustration, I entered a year-long coaching program just to figure out how to run a coaching business. Through that program I was given an opportunity to get a certification around your relationship with money. PERFECT, I thought…a business in a box that I can turn around and teach to others.

Well after 5 minutes, I was humbled! I realized that was exactly what I needed to heal my money story!

Through the intensive 5 month program I started peeling away layers of beliefs and mindsets that I had accumulated over the years. Money meant overwhelm, anxiety, materialism, over indulgence, polluting the purity of what I loved to do and boredom (remember, I am an artist!). If money meant all that to me, why in the world would I want it close to me? As soon as money came in, I would mindlessly spend to get it out of my life. As soon as success came into my life I would self-sabotage those opportunities.

It was time to create a new story!

We all unconsciously absorb values, mindsets and beliefs around money from our families, environment, and media. All of our decisions conscious or unconscious are based on those beliefs and mindsets.

> **"How you do money is how you do everything."**
>
> ~ Kendall SummerHawk

Money is at the core of almost every decision we make in our lives from the foods we eat, where we vacation, where we send our kids to school, what clothes we wear, and where we live to name a few. Our money beliefs, stories and feelings of what we deserve secretly control the decisions we make and yes it shows up in our business and careers.

These powerful beliefs determine how much we have, how much revenue we bring in, how profitable our business is, and how much success we allow into our life. We unconsciously and consciously make decisions based on our mindsets. In order to make new decisions we need a new way of seeing ourselves, new mindsets, and a new set of beliefs of what is truly possible.

Generally men see money as a transaction and women see it as an emotional exchange. For most women, money is an emotional exchange of worth. Most financial workshops have not taken this simple difference into consideration. Which means, most women have not been given the tools to make clear, insightful, money decisions or to feel certain, confident and even secure about how to earn, own and make decisions about money.

It is not because of intelligence. Women simply have not been given the tools to make decisions on the one key ingredient it takes to having a business: money!

When you are hooked into the negative triggers around money it can show up in a variety of ways in your business or career:

- Undercharging
- Over-delivering
- Bartering/trading
- Low enrollment
- Hesitating to invest in growth
- Hesitating to make offers
- Not closing sales
- Not asking for a raise
- Not asking for referrals
- Believing people won't pay more
- Paying too much for support or not getting enough value
- No collaboration partners or hesitating to collaborate
- Tolerating clients who miss a payment or drop out of programs
- Feeling invisible or not making a name for oneself
- Having arguments about money with spouse/partner
- Being passed over for promotion
- Not getting a new job opportunity

When you unhook from the emotional pull of negative money triggers then you can powerfully:

• Make offers
• Close sales
• Collaborate with exciting partners
• Ask for referrals
• Make a name for yourself
• Own your value
• Create financial harmony with your partner/spouse
• Invest in growing your business/career

The work I do is based on my 3 core empowerment beliefs.

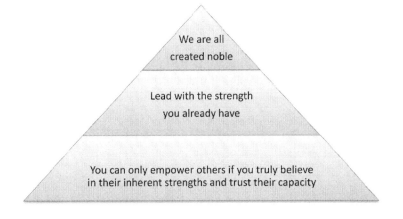

As a Money Mindset business coach, I love empowering others. I approach my clients knowing with certainty that they already have the strengths, gifts and talents inside of them. It is not an approach of "lack." My job is a simple process of identifying my clients' money strengths to co-creating a new mindset so THEY can courageously step into making the most powerful decision for their business and career. In this way they start creating a new money story and healing money legacy they have inherited. They powerfully step into being the CEO of their business and career.

So let's get started in creating a new mindset in order to make the next powerful choice for your business or career.

Step One: Money Brilliance

Let us start by identifying what your strengths and gifts are around money. I call these your money brilliance. Lead with the strength you already have. Everyone has strengths in how they relate to money. It is simply identifying them and leveraging them to make your decisions. Your strengths are the tip of the spear to pierce through the challenges most effectively and efficiently. This helps accelerate the growth of your business and career.

With my clients, I start with a highly accurate proprietary money assessment that specifically highlights their strengths, gifts and natural capacity with money. For you to get started, I have highlighted a handful of qualities for you to consider.

Quick Money Assessment

Do you give amazing value?
Do you love empowering others?
Do you see possibilities?
Do you love innovating new and exciting growth opportunities?
Do you love creating an empire where everyone thrives?

If you said yes to any of these, they are some of the amazing qualities, gifts and strengths you have with money that you bring to the table in your business and career. Congratulations!

What then causes challenges? An imbalance of strengths.

For instance: You give amazing value and love creating an empire where everyone thrives. However you concentrate on giving amazing value and not setting up strong boundaries, agreements and contracts in your business. So what happens? Most likely you will over deliver, under charge, barter and give away your services for free. Now if you start concentrating on also creating an empire where everyone thrives, then you will create stronger boundaries with your time, charge what you feel is fair for your services, and not barter or give away your services for free just to "prove" your value. You are still giving amazing value which helps your clients or your company to thrive but you are also being compensated so that you will also thrive.

Step Two: New Mindset

Next, let's co-create a new mindset. This is based on 3 important questions.

Value: Why is this important to me?

Identity: Who do I see myself as?

Belief: What do I believe is possible?

In order to create alignment and harmony with the strengths and natural way you connect with money you need a new mindset. Your new mindsets are based on what you value, your identity and your belief of what is possible. Carol DeWyck of Stanford University, one of the leading researchers in motivation, basically says that our mindset determines the level of our achievements.

I will guide you through a new mindset. Fill in this sentence with words that feel empowering. You can change the sentence structure if needed.

The more_____I get with money, the more I _____myself.

Examples of Empowering Words

Abundance	Courage
Powerful	Privilege
Empowering	Prosper
Security	Rich
Respect	Accumulate
Resilience	Save
Persevere	Wealth

Now that you have created your "new" mindset, answer these questions for yourself.

Value: What do you value about having money in your life? What does it mean for your business/relationships/career?

Identity: What kind of business woman or professional woman do you see yourself as with this new mindset?

Belief: What do you feel is possible in your business, career or life with this new mindset?

Step Three: Powerful Decision

I truly believe that the mind cannot be fooled. You need to give it evidence that YOU ARE being successful. The best way to do that is to get into action. No matter how small. Then your brain downloads that you ARE. It does not matter if you decide to save $5 a week or $1000. You ARE saving when you follow through with that decision. Your strengths plus your new mindsets allow you to make powerful decisions in your business. Money is the fuel for your business and career. Money is a form of energy. Without money you simply have a hobby or a volunteer job.

What is the most powerful decision you can make based on this new mindset?

The powerful decisions that you make for your business or career fall into 3 categories. These categories are interconnected and feed into one another.

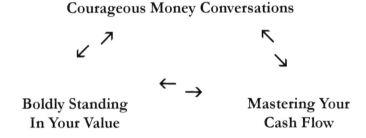

Courageous Money Conversations

Boldly Standing In Your Value

Mastering Your Cash Flow

~ Courageous Money Conversations ~

I call these courageous because when you start engaging in conversations that change the status quo as most money conversations do, it takes courage. You are redefining yourself and the relationship. These conversations are not for the faint of heart! Sometimes they bring up fears of rejection, acceptance or derivability. They are a process of empowering your voice, boundaries and integrity.

~ Boldly Standing in Your Value ~

You are unique. There is not one way to express or stand in the value you bring to your clients or company. It is only when you are not being authentic in whom you are that you will seem aggressive, pushy, bossy or even a ...! Do not follow formulas that do not align with who you are and how you want to show up in the world. Leveraging your unique strengths and gifts around money is a highly empowering way to stay connected with the best way you can show up for your business and career. Standing in your value influences how you promote and market yourself and how you show up at networking events, interviews and company meetings, and even how you present, speak and deliver to your clients or at work.

~ Mastering Your Cash Flow ~

Numbers tell a story. Sometimes that story can mean embarrassment, judgment, feelings of inadequacy, or I "should have more." Sometimes it is just not feeling connected as to why you have to look at those numbers. It is important to connect with your strengths and gifts around money to answer the big "money why" in your business or career. This creates a meaningful connection of why you need to track your money, look at your accounts and set numerical goals to achieve the cash flow. If there is any resistance or conflict in wanting to look at these important numbers in your business it is simply because you are not emotionally connected to the "why." Once again, it has nothing to do with intelligence or even not knowing that you need to do it.

Having courageous money conversations, boldly standing in your value and mastering your cash flow are interrelated. They actually flow one into the other at no matter what point you start. The more you look at the numbers in your business and courageously have the conversations that are needed the more you can actually stand in your value powerfully, authentically and boldly. Here are some examples:

Courageous Money Conversations	Boldly Standing in Your Value	Mastering Your Cash Flow
• Stating your fees • Negotiating with vendor • Asking for a raise or negotiating your salary • Discussing expenditures with your spouse/partner • Asking a client to get current with their payments	• Stating and listing the value your services give to your clients or company • Asking for new opportunities/referrals • Saying "no" • Being detached from the "nos" • Establishing yourself as the "go to"expert	• Knowing the numbers in your specific business • Knowing how many clients you need, how you will get them, and by what date • Regularly tracking money coming in and going out • Having enrolling conversations • Knowing when to outsource

~ Wrap Up ~

Now we are going to tie up everything that we have done together in one last exercise. This will touch upon each category of decisions that you will need to make in your business/career.

Your new money mindset:

The more_____I get with money , the more I _____myself.

1. What is one money conversation you will now have?
2. List 2 ways that your services or expertise is unique.
3. As the CEO of your business/career what is one financial detail you need to know?

Mamak Charepoo believes that everyone has the right to feel safe to flourish. Her own journey in shifting money beliefs that were sabotaging her success and prosperity has inspired her to work with organizations, groups and individuals in promoting and presenting the value of their product and services, having money conversations with ease, and creating service structures that are aligned with their values and goals. Mamak has a Master of Fine Arts from Arizona State University and a Master of Music from Carnegie Mellon University. She has been a collaborator, teacher, trainer, and speaker in her music, children's class coordinator and coaching careers. She has been interviewed on Powerful Women Revealed radio and PACTV, and has been highlighted by popular HBR blogger, Whitney Johnson's Dare to Dream blog. She is a Nurtured Heart Approach® Advanced Trainer, and Sacred Money Archetype® Certified Coach. She is a member of IAWC and Pod Leader for Believe Inspire Grow. Mamak Charepoo, MM, MFA, NHA® Advanced Trainer, SMA® Certified Coach, (617)959-9581, www.charepoocoaching.com.

Chapter 8

Finding Your Life's Work
from the Inside Out

Louise Talotta, CPC

"When we come from our passions and strengths, natural motivation and results follow." ~ J.M., Banking Executive – New York

What do you want from your work? How do you want to feel about the work you do? Your answers to these questions are the greatest gifts you can give yourself before you leap into deciding your life's work.

This chapter is targeted for young people early in their careers but insightful for any age. It raises awareness for who you are and what you want and walks you through the search process. When you make choices that consider your natural strengths, interests, and goals and priorities; then motivation, increased energy and happiness are the gifts back to you.

Did you know that the average person spends over 90,000 hours at work over their lifetime? How do you want to fill that time? The choices are yours. There are many possibilities and they change as you change. This is especially important for young graduates because career thinking and decisions in the first ten years of entering the workplace have everything to do with how careers develop later.

> *"By the time people reach mid-career, nearly 70 percent are in a job that isn't in alignment with their talents or sense of purpose. Feeling trapped in the wrong profession, many people will choose to stay put and fake it, end up job hopping or go back to school without comprehending that the fix for their dissatisfaction is to use their innate talents rather than struggle to overcome their perceived weaknesses."*
> ~ Anthony Spadafore, Pathfinders

When your life's work is what you love to do in the environment that sustains you, then accomplishment, income, recognition and connections will fulfill you more than you can ever imagine.

How do your early career choices set the path for your future? As your career becomes more seasoned, how will you apply what you have learned about yourself to influence new choices? Does your work support you to be at your happiest and best?

Three Common Limiting Beliefs about Work

1. A lot of money has been spent on my education and I don't have a lot of experience. I need to find a career that matches my education so I will be hired.

Fact: All education and experience contributes to our knowledge, growth and perspectives. Education prompts learning and growth and expands perspectives and opportunities. Nearly half (47 percent) of college-educated workers said their first job after college was not related to their college major.

Tip: Reflect on your educational experience and identify your interests and strengths along with the areas of study you enjoyed the most. Think about past knowledge and skills you can draw upon; these are transferable skills. Reflect on the similarities between your passions, strengths, education and experience before applying for jobs to understand all of your qualities. Employers want team players who possess attributes that blend with and contribute to their products, services and culture,…the most important qualities employers seek are basic teamwork, problem-solving skills and the ability to plan and prioritize.

2. I can't say I am sure this is a great job, but it's a paycheck so I'm lucky to have that.

Fact: As we limit our beliefs, we limit ourselves. When we settle for work that doesn't give us what we need, we don't bring our best to it. Happiness then diminishes in the other areas of our lives because we bring less of ourselves.

Tip: Check-in and reflect upon your current satisfaction levels with these eight parts of your life. For each area, assign a number from 0 -10. (10 is your highest satisfaction level.) (1) Home and Environment; (2) Job; (3) Relationships; (4) Finances; (5) Health; (6) Family and Friends; (7) Growth and Learning; and (8) Fun and Leisure. How do your 'scores' feel to you? Surprised? How is your choice for work adding or lessening satisfaction in these areas? If you make changes in your work, how could other areas of your life be more satisfying? Reflect on whether experiencing enjoyable activities and hobbies will help balance work or whether you are ready to take a leap to something different.

3. I've already put time into my education or work so if I change now it will be wasted or I will 'go backwards.'

Fact: Although there are challenges when seeking new careers or employers, many success stories abound when people take the risk for happiness. Sylvester Stallone was 30 before he wrote and starred in 'Rocky'. Danny Aiello began acting at age 40. Julia Child began to cook in her fifties. Colonel Sanders founded his franchise in his sixties and Frank McCourt published his first book, 'Angela's Ashes' when he was 66, obtaining a Pulitzer Prize. Grandma Moses began her painting career in her eighties.

Tip: Define your personal 'brand' and stay aware of the work, environment and people you enjoy. Reflect on what gives or drains your energy. By understanding the pieces that bring satisfaction, you will make better decisions for what you want. Every change brings you forward with a new experience that fills the space of what has been let go. Your transferable skills and qualities can be leveraged to change industries, environments or other aspects of your work. Athletes coach, engineers invent, sales people change products, artists design websites; the possibilities are endless. The roles we choose become opportunities to contribute, shape and influence our individual brand.

Live forward into the life you were meant to live. Time will not wait for you.

Happiness is the culmination of results from every decision made across all the parts of life.

What if:

⇨ You believed you could love your work and that the work, place and people helped you thrive?

⇨ You felt you REALLY deserved to receive all you want from your work and that it was possible?

⇨ You could understand what makes you happy early in your life so you keep getting more of that?

⇨ You knew of and practiced a different 'formula' for finding your jobs and careers to make this more likely?

JobSeek© is an easy tool that helps you tap into the knowledge of others, gather personal insights and walk through a 7 step 'formula' for finding your life's work 'from the inside out.'

JobSeek'© Steps!

Step 1: Journal – Ask these questions of someone over the age of forty:

⇨ When you were little, what did you want to be when you grew up?

⇨ When you were in high school, what subjects did you like the best?

⇨ If you went on for further education or training, what did you study or major in?

⇨ What do you do for work now?

⇨ What have you learned that you would like to share with me?

Watch their pauses. Notice reactions. Listen to what is said and what is not. Chances are they intuitively enjoyed certain activities or studies. They may have used natural strengths or studied areas they admired someone else for. There is no right or wrong answer. Make notes in a journal to enrich your ideas. When you understand the journeys of others you learn from their experiences and raise awareness for your own questions, approaches and decisions.

Step 2: Obtain information about yourself to increase your self-awareness:

⇨ Make a List about YOU: Think about the jobs and activities you have experienced. Make a list of what you liked, why you liked it, the strengths and qualities you demonstrated and what others liked about you and your contributions. These are gems that can guide you in your process because they stood out to others.

⇨ Visualization Activity: Take a deep breath in and let it out slowly. Repeat this until you are feeling calm and centered. Imagine yourself in your perfect job.

- What is it?
- Where are you?
- What is the value from what you are doing?
- What are the people like?
- What is the value you are receiving?
- How do you feel?

As information presents itself, refine the vision for your perfect role until it feels right for you.

⇨ Research self-assessments and books to define your strengths and interests. The time you take to learn about yourself is the best investment you can make before you start the job search. When you work naturally from your place of strengths and interests, the learning and satisfaction you receive from your job is priceless.

Great and time-proven books and assessments include:

- Book: 'What color is Your Parachute?', Richard N. Bolles
- Book and online assessment: 'Strengths Finder 2.0', Tom Rath
- Book and online assessment: 'Emotional Intelligence 2.0', Travis Bradberry and Jean Greaves
- Assessment: Myers-Briggs Type Indicator (MBTI)
- Assessment: Strong Interest Inventory (SII)

Step 3: Background - Research job openings and know employer practices.

⇨ Now that you have collected some information about yourself, check with family, friends, online and newspapers to see what opportunities are available. Think about your priorities: Do you want work that provides experience in a new area or fits a specific need? Would working for a company you are familiar with be the answer? Do you want to stay local or are you willing to move? What schedule and location fits your personal life? What is most important to you in the job and in the place you work? Reflect on previous notes and lists you have made and compare your priorities to what is available.

- Research opportunities and what they require. Create a list of openings you are interested in and include the information that matches your priorities. Many companies have their own online job application process. Websites used frequently by employers and jobseekers include:
- Indeed.com
- Monster.com
- CareerBuilder.com
- Talk to people you or your family and friends know who do similar work or work in places you are considering.

• Find out what you can about different employers: research them and understand their business and culture. Most have websites, check them out thoroughly.

Step 4: Strategy – Create your winning strategy and plan for the job you want.

➪ Design your approach by reviewing requirements for the jobs that interest you along with their required education, experience and characteristics. Compare your strengths, knowledge, background and interests with the role. Determine your unique value and how that role will satisfy you according to your priorities. Read job descriptions carefully for location, hours, travel needs and expected knowledge and tasks that match your strengths, interests and priorities. Employers are often willing to overlook required degrees or technical training if you have demonstrated similar experience. Think about how your strengths and knowledge will help the employer if they choose you. Note whether you have personal contacts and talk to them about the possibilities. They may have insights into the job you are considering. Prioritize your choices and note designated job codes. Check your sources at the beginning and end of each week.

Step 5: Empower – Create your resume and develop behavioral interviewing skills.

➪ Build your powerful resume. Reflect on your insights, education, experience and skills and see how they match to the employer's needs. Avoid 'force-fitting' to what is being asked because it cannot be sustained long-term. When what you give is balanced with what you receive, you and your work is at its best.

• Match the employer requested education, experience, knowledge, skills and needs with what you have to offer for each item. (If 40% of the time you are required to use a skill that doesn't give you satisfaction, you might get the role but do you really want it?) The hardest part about searching for a job is keeping yourself from settling for what you can do vs. what you want to do.

⇨ Top resume best practices include:

• Appropriate personal email address and telephone contact information is placed at the top.
• In a designated top section, list bullets that best summarize your experience and qualities. You need to grab the reader's attention within 30 seconds. Companies screen first for what they don't want before they evaluate those that are left. They decide quickly whether to keep reading or go to the next applicant.
• Use action-oriented words to describe your previous roles; "Created...Led...Designed."
• Keep content to two pages and do not include references unless they are asked for.
• Choose 3 supportive references that will be able to describe how you fit the needs of the role you are applying for. They will also speak to your character and should be comfortable answering questions from prospective employers. Once they agree, create a separate reference sheet. Place your name and contact heading at the top. List reference names with contact information and a brief description of your relationship to them. Bring these to your interviews along with extra copies of your resume.

⇨ Practice behavioral interviewing skills – interviewing styles vary but they all want to see if you fit personally and professionally. Behavioral interviewing is commonly practiced to bring out the stories of how you achieved something rather than just knowing what it was. This technique tells the interviewer how you approach challenges, accomplish work and interact with others.

• Based on the job you are interested in, reflect on achievements that showcase similar abilities. Learn more about behavioral interviewing and practice with someone who can ask questions like: "Tell me about a time when…How did you…What was difficult about…..Describe how you decided to…"

- Be active, not passive during interviews; listen and ask. Listen for their problems and share your relevant insights. Employers value problem-solvers. Discover how the people and culture will support you to be successful. Since the majority of employees leave jobs because of the relationship they have with their direct boss, probe thoroughly to understand style and management skills. You are deciding whether you really want this role. Ask interviewers for their business cards for later thank-you emails.

Step 6: Engage – Follow up with references, interviewers and networks

⇨ Communication and follow-up is key to showing appreciation and staying connected:

- When an interview date is set, reach out and inform your contacts. They may be able to meet you prior to the interview and assist you with insights.
- Following your interviews, call your references and make them aware they may be contacted and thank them.
- Send thank-you emails to all of your interviewers but do not contact them directly to ask about your hiring status unless instructed to do so.
- Follow protocol regarding how and who to contact after your interviews. A follow-up email is appropriate if you have not heard in two weeks. Generally, the company contact for the role will only call the person selected.

Step 7: Keep – Take care of yourself, keep your confidence and continue to search for other roles.

⇨ Stay connected to hobbies and interests that keep you centered and look to family and friends for support. Attend career fairs and talk with recruiters. Stay focused on your approach and actions and trust that if you are doing all you can, a great role will come to you.

⇨ Seek additional expertise and support such as a Life and Career coach to support your 'forward' thinking and actions. They are your champions and through their powerful questions, objectivity and insights you can search for the work you love feeling supported and confident.

Maintain a positive vision for your future and feel gratitude for those who support you. Never let fear or assumptions be your guide. Stay open to new information that presents itself - it could be an opportunity in disguise. Check in with your heart and natural intuition and be honest with the feelings that come up for you. Know that you have much to offer because each person's gifts are unique. You deserve the work you love.

Coming from within by fully being who you are
allows you to expand outside into the world
to fully do what brings you happiness.

Louise Talotta, CPC, of BridgeLight Coaching, LLC is a certified life and business coach with over 30 years of experience in health care and Fortune 100 companies. Her long professional career allowed her to work with many leaders and employees who navigated obstacles and strove to make a difference in their work while trying to balance full and busy lives. Her coaching business was born from the passion of helping people evaluate and reframe their perspectives to expand into their possibilities. She is accredited by the International Coaching Academy, ICA, for life and business coaching. Her educational background at the University of Connecticut includes a bachelor's degree with honors in organizational management and a Business Mastery certification. Her education and background in Human Resources, leadership and strategic planning brings expertise and insights for her clients through in-person, telephone or online sessions. By bringing intuitive coaching and people skills to her clients, they are supported to reach amazing goals. http://www.bridgelightcoaching.com, bridgelightcoaching@yahoo.com.

Chapter 9

Spiritual Transformation
Balancing Body, Mind and Spirit

Ellen Gilhooly, RP, MPC

What is a spiritual transformation and how does it relate to a person's journey? In order to define spiritual transformation, one must have an understanding of the word spirituality. Spirituality is more than organized religion and prayer; it includes introspection, a person's values, and beliefs. Spirituality is about finding one's purpose or meaning to their existence. An individual's spirituality can include prayer, affirmations, and a physical practice such as yoga or walking meditations. Finding the light within each of us and the ability to live in harmony with the outside forces of everyday life is the basis of any spiritual transformation.

Body, Mind and Spirit

There are three key areas of focus for a spiritual transformation; body, mind, and spirit. In order to transform one's thoughts, behaviors and health there needs to be a balance of these areas. If any one of these is off balance than one's entire existence is off. Once an individual begins to transform their thoughts and behaviors the body will begin to heal itself, because the body always wants to be in harmony or in a state of homeostasis. In order to achieve this state, there are tools which can be incorporated into one's life such as; writing in a journal, getting out into nature, and paying attention to negative thoughts. Our bodies are wonderful instruments and respond accordingly when treated like a temple. This means feeding our creative side, honoring our inner spirit and listening to the messages our bodies will give us when they become unbalanced.

I believe we have the natural ability to heal our bodies by tapping into our inner light or our inner spirit which connects us to the power of the universe. Reiki is an energy healing modality that helps us fine-tune our intuition and inner spirit. Sometimes we live our lives without listening to our intuition. In fact, when we are born our intuition is uninhibited. As we grow and our egos develop our intuition gets quieter. Reiki is the tool that brings power to our intuition which in turn brightens our inner spirit. Reiki helps us and our clients connect to our inner spirit.

Connect to the Universe with Reiki

All of us carry within us the ability to heal ourselves. Some people can access their inner spirit through prayer or meditation, without Reiki. However, I have found it does help clients access their connection to the universe with very little or no effort on their part during a Reiki session. Reiki can be used as a complement to any current spiritual or personal-growth path to transformation.

Reiki helps clients progress toward wholeness and opens them up to the universal life-force energy. Reiki takes clients to a safe place, a place of trusting that their lives will be ok. Reiki makes clients more aware of the universal life-force energy, which helps them as life throws its twist and turns. Reiki puts clients in a state of relaxation that allows ideas to come to them because they are in a state of non-resistance. Reiki creates a sense of peace and harmony between the client and the universe, making it one of the best ways to kick off your spiritual transformation.

I use Reiki on myself almost every day as a way to quiet my mind and relax my body so my inner spirit can help me achieve homeostasis. Since I began a daily Reiki practice, I have less colds, and my health has been excellent.

The Power of Journaling

The next important tool to incorporate on a spiritual transformation is a journal. The first step to writing in a journal is to release the idea and the energy surrounding it, that your thoughts or emotions need to be hidden from others. This will release any negative feelings of fear and secrecy which tend to inhibit the free flow of ideas and thoughts. The second step is to release the negative thoughts you may have about perfect spelling, handwriting or grammar, there is no need to be correct and no place for perfection in a journal. Thoughts are in our minds, and the best way to discharge the negative ones is to give them words and to put them on paper. Think of it as a release valve on the pressure cooker, opening it is a way to bring balance to mind, body and spirit.

Over the years I have learned the power of writing in a journal. I have let go of the behavior and thought patterns that my journals need to be hidden from others. I have allowed the art of trusting my loved ones and often leave my journal on my night stand, or on my desk. There is nothing to hide; therefore the energy of trust surrounds my journals. In our family we honor each other's right to privacy. My husband and I have always respected our children's right to privacy and they in return give it back. This allows me to write freely in my journal, which allows a very important outlet for my spirit and my emotional health. This directly and positively impacts my physical health.

I always encourage my clients to get a journal and to write down their thoughts, desires, dreams, and goals. Most importantly, I ask them to write down their feelings of failure, frustration, anger, fear and anxiety. When they don't know what to write I encourage them to just do a free write. A free write is the act of writing whatever comes to their minds, to their hearts or to their spirits. I explain to them that it may have no rhyme or reason to it, but the key is to keep writing. I instruct them to use a timer when doing a free write to help set a boundary. Start with five minutes and just start writing what comes to your mind. This will help you get into a continuous expression of thought and open up a pathway for your spirit to strengthen. I also let them know that sometimes my mind would work faster than my fingers and so I have found over the years I can type faster than I can write. If you are more comfortable with typing, then by all means use a computer. If however, there are times when typing on a computer seems too impersonal to me or I want to write outside in the woods or by the water, I honor that and these are the times I use a journal.

My journals are like having a good friend always available when I need them. All my journals have something special about them. For example, I have one that my husband gave to me. He enjoys wood carving, which feeds his inner spirit and his strong creative side. It is one of his many outlets that keep his mind, body and spirit in balance. For the front of the journal, he carved a dragonfly into a piece of wood, because he knows I love dragonflies. He took a regular journal and put a wood cover on top. I have been writing in it for over two years and I am about half way through it. There are times when I will pick up a different journal and write in it for a period of time. I always use the format of putting the date and the day of the week when starting my journal entry. Sometimes, my journal entries can fill up three or four pages, on other days I can only write a few lines. Whatever the day brings I write what I can and let it go. There are days where I have stopped midsentence because I was interrupted. I have learned to honor my process and my journal writing. There is no right or wrong way to use this tool; however it is very important to use it as a support mechanism during your spiritual transformation.

I keep all my journals. At times, I have gone back to read my journals. I find that reading past journal entries is a form of healing. A journal entry may be about one of my dreams. It could be about describing my point of view regarding a struggle with my family or friends. It might be about my frustration in a lack of direction in my life. Some entries are very benign. Today I did this thing or that thing. The important thing is that I wrote. There are times when days, weeks or months go by and I remove writing from my daily routine. I honor those times by not judging my need to put my writing aside. It is about the journey and there is no right or wrong way to do it. My spirit knows when I need to write and when to put it on the back burner.

The Law of Attraction

Our thoughts are very powerful. We are made up of energy which cannot be destroyed only changed. Our thoughts are energy. The things we spend time thinking about set our intention or our vibration. These intentions and vibrations are sent out to the universe. The universe is loaded with energy and gives back to us the same energy we sent out. This is the Law of Attraction. The Law of Attraction is the flow of energy between each person and the universe. For example, positive thoughts and positive vibrations sent out to the universe will return positive results and positive vibrations. Positive attracts positive whereas negative attracts negative.

I was first introduced to the Law of Attraction in 2005. The first book I picked up was *Ask And It Is Given* by Esther and Jerry Hicks. I was skeptical about the concepts in the book. I was even more skeptical when I found out Esther channeled a spirit named Abraham to give the messages about the Law of Attraction. I had gone to a medium before, in fact I had several inspiring and comforting experiences connecting to souls or getting messages through mediums. Nonetheless, it did take some time for me to truly feel comfortable with the process of Esther channeling Abraham. I needed to get past my resistance which allowed me to accept Esther's gift was genuine. Once I did, the messages and concepts of the Law of Attraction became part of my spiritual practice.

Over time I have incorporated many of the teachings of Abraham. For example, Law of Abundance is something I have struggled with for many years. I don't feel worthy of abundance and my childhood experience taught me I would never have abundance. Nine years later, I have reaped the benefits of working the Law of Attraction and the art of allowing abundance to come into my life. The crucial function to incorporating the Law of Attraction into my life was saying the affirmations and then being conscious of how it feels in my body when I say those words. For example: I would say this affirmation, "I spend money wisely, I always have as much as I need," then I take a deep breath. As I breathe, I take notice of where I feel sensations in my body. Do I feel tension or stress? Do I feel calm, peaceful and excited? I have learned the important element is to allow myself to feel the happiness, power, and peacefulness in my body. I instruct my clients, "Feel it in your body as if you already spend money wisely and have as much as you need." I used to cry and worry about having enough money, which made me feel sick to my stomach and sometimes my heart would race. But now, by using this technique I let go of the worry and allow myself to feel peaceful and happy. The results are my body feels calm, there have been less bills and the money is there when I need it.

The Law of Gratitude is an essential component to acceptance and success of the Law of Attraction. Law of Gratitude is the process of being grateful for the things you have now. There are a few actions I use to ignite and fuel the energy of gratitude. I recommend doing these steps daily until it becomes an unconscious behavior. The first step is to say twenty times out loud the words, "Thank you." The next step is to write down a list of gratitude items, we call them "gratitudes." For example: I am so grateful for a warm house on a cold day. I am grateful for my new puppy Riley. Write down as many as you like. I have a separate gratitude journal or you can use this exercise as part of your daily journal entry. As you write each gratitude item, say the words out loud then take a deep breath to see if you can feel a sense of gratitude in your body. Don't skip this step. It is a very important tool to connect your body, mind and spirit. It is also very important to the process of igniting the Law of Attraction in your life.

Once you have completed these ground-work steps, the next step actually begins the process of the Law of Attraction, with the art of allowing. Write down all the things you want to come into your life. The most important step is to write the gratitudes as if you already have them. For instance, if I want to become a well-known author and motivational speaker, my gratitude would be written as, "I am so grateful for the successful books I have written and published." Or "I am grateful for a full audience at my speaking engagement." Next, I would breathe deeply after I have said the words out loud and feel the deep gratitude in my body.

Experiencing the feeling in our bodies is the most important step to attracting our desires. It is the action of feeling the positive sensation in our bodies and sending positive energy out to the universe.

The Law of Attraction is a powerful tool in anyone's spiritual transformation. It provides tangible action steps on how to view the world as a cup half-full, rather than half-empty.

Animal Totems

As I was going through my own spiritual and personal growth transformation, I was introduced to the American Indian practice of Animal Medicine. I specifically found comfort in a practice of using animal cards to receive messages from the universe. This provided me guidance and answers to the daily challenges I was facing. Animal Medicine has become a very powerful tool in my spiritual practice. I have found the animals who cross my path give me information regarding the current challenges I am facing in my life. For example, if I am out on a walk at the reservoir and a deer crosses my path this usually means I need to be a little gentler with myself and the others involved in my current challenge. Or it can mean I need to be sensitive to the fear that is surrounding my current challenge.

My most recent experience did occur at the reservoir during a time where I was feeling a lot of fear about who I was and how others felt about me. As I began my walk, a deer came out of the woods into my path and stood about 20 to 30 feet in front of me. She was beautiful and confident. She clearly was not afraid of me. I was stunned and a sense of fear came over me. Was there something wrong with the deer? Should I run the other way? How come she is so bold and confident? As we stood there staring at one another, she casually walked to the other side of the path and began to eat the leaves on the bush. She would look over at me but never once did she show any fear. I decided to continue my walk. The deer kept munching on her leaves and at one point we stared at each other. I was so close to her that if I had reached out my right hand I could have touched her. As I continued on my walk I decided to stay with the feeling of being one with nature. I enjoyed the moment and the sense of peace I felt in my body. My intuition and my inner spirit became more dominant than my ego. This provided the ability for me to get the following message, "Don't be afraid, there is nothing scary about your heart or spirit."

Another time, I saw a bald eagle at the reservoir land in a tree. As I approached the tree, I watched the bald eagle sway with the wind. The white of the feathers on his head was very striking. I was filled with gratitude as I thought, "How was I so fortunate that this magnificent creature showed itself to me?" I stood there for nearly five minutes watching him. At one point, the eagle and I locked eyes and I felt a bolt of energy shoot through my body. Within minutes, this beautiful, brave, wise creature took flight right over my head. I watched it soar over the water and saw its beautiful white tail and strong wings against the bright blue sky. Then it flew out of sight. I noticed how I felt in my body. I felt strong, courageous and free. I felt free to be the person I am meant to be. I felt brave about the steps I was taking towards my dream of being a writer, a healer, and a spiritual mentor. The bald eagle was a gift from the universe and I will cherish it forever. I went home to look up what the bald eagle represented. Most websites say the Bald Eagle medicine teaches our spirit the power of being a loner with awesome grace and beauty and that eagle medicine people have large Spirits which may intimidate many people. The Bald Eagle medicine may mean you will have amazing visions, keen insight, heroic stamina and the highest of ascension towards understanding and attaining Great Spirit. This bald eagle was clearly a spirit guide I needed to see.

Sometimes during a session with a client, I will perform guided meditations as a way to gather more information and guidance regarding the current issue we are working. As the client begins to quiet their mind and pay attention to their breathing and their body sensations, I will ask them to call for an image. The image may be an animal, a color or an object. Once the client visualizes the image, we go through three questions, "Ask the image for a message. Ask the image what it needs from you. Tell the image what you need from it." Most often, the image is an animal and the animal always gives the client a message which provides additional support or information for their current issue. I use my animal medicine cards as a reference and I encourage my clients to get a set of these cards or to use the internet to get the spiritual meaning for their animal guides. My favorite book of reference is *Medicine Cards: The Discovery of Power Through the Ways of Animals* by Jamie Sams and David Carson.

I help my clients find ways to thrive rather than merely survive. I help them to achieve their highest potential and find purpose and meaning in their existence. I help place them on their spiritual journey connecting their minds, bodies, and spirits; taking the essential steps to their spiritual transformation.

You came into this world with a glowing bright white inner light, an inner spirit that will connect you to the universe. It is this inner light which helps a person achieve their highest potential and find the purpose or meaning in their life.

Ellen Gilhooly's experience includes five years of Body Center Gestalt training from the Hartford Family Institute and ten years' experience as a Master Reiki Practitioner. She recently completed a Master's Degree in Pastoral Counseling. For the last 26 years, Ellen worked for a fortune 500 Healthcare Company as a Senior Director managing three technology teams as well as acting as a Chief of Staff for an Executive Director. During her career, she had the opportunity to hold positions in Human Resources and mentored several managers to enhance their leadership skills. Ellen created Partners In Spirit to help people see through their chaos in order to discover and create a clear vision for their lives. She helps guide and support people to make each day a blessing and to embrace their individual life force. Most importantly, she helps an individual identify the times when they are operating more from their ego which stifles their inner spirit. Our ego is to help us to survive, not thrive. Ellen believes most people want to thrive not just survive. Ellen Gilhooly, partnersinspirit@yahoo.com.

Chapter 10

The Hunger to Be a Leader

Tom Bohinc, MBA, CPCC

"The things worth reading about… feel almost beyond description at the start and are, because of that, frightening."

~ Douglas Coupland

L eadership secretly attracts all of us, not only the extroverts and the ambitious. Please, take time to trust that instinct. And please, take actions to build your leadership awareness and to realize leadership as part of your purpose.

The path 'to arrive at leadership' holds contrasting and paradoxical experiences.

The path winds through spectacular and inspiring terrain with solid ground for your footing and with solid grasps for where your footing is unsure.

The path is easy because you have natural ability, though some of it may be unfamiliar to you.

The path is easy when you expand the range and assumptions of your resourcefulness.

The path is easy when you connect to inner strengths such as joy, assuredness, and worthiness.

In contrast, some of the terrain is threatening and even seems monstrous. We can imagine ourselves suffering a mishap or two. And, there are times when you find neither footing nor hand-holds to support you.

Finding your way to your own leadership requires letting go of some habits of mind. The letting go may seem scary, like that first step across a gap on the trail, or the first time you rode your bike, or jumped into the pool. The intent of this chapter is to radicalize your view of leadership and see it as something compelling and accessible. I want to awaken your belief and conviction in your unique calling to leadership, and to instill intentionality in your choices for your achievement of leadership.

Shifting Your Focus

The CEO for a high-growth media company asked me how to shift his key executive team "to lead more." They were gifted and trusted resources. They were smart, caring and hardworking. But, he felt, they left opportunities to contribute on the table. And, their ability to sustain momentum and quality were not strong enough that the CEO could step back from day-to-day activities. The company was thriving, but nearing its capacity to continue to grow. In order to continue growing, he wanted to shift his own engagement and trust that the company would run well and prosper.

A senior executive in a large and high-powered financial company asked me how to approach his own strategy for engaging his peers during the shift in market-strategy and operations that the company was going through. "I would like to come through this having contributed more than making my own operation successful in the transition."

My answer to both of these executives, one who wanted to shift his team, and one that wanted to extend his leadership to his peers, was that the best strategy was to shift perspectives on their purpose in the organization. The best shift is to establish a 'creative and innovative climate' in themselves, and then in their organization, and their operations. I told them that the most effective option for their transformation would be a program of experiences, reflection, and intention that included personal and group coaching.

There is a very, very subtle point here. If you are going to shift your effectiveness, then you have to shift your focus. To shift your focus you have to shift yourself. The shift is from your distractions of living in the past or counting too much on the future, or counting too much on something outside of yourself. The shift is to your authenticity, your whole intelligence (this is something specific), your commitment to choice in action, your own self and systems awareness, your relationship to others and the world, and in my experience one of the most surprising insights: your relationship to fear, uncertainty and doubt in juxtaposition to your purpose.

What most people do is stop

"There is something in every one of you that waits and listens for the sound of the genuine in yourself….. if you cannot hear it, you will all of your life spend your days on the ends of strings that somebody else pulls."
~ Howard Thurman

A Set of Patterns

The last thirty years of research in adult growth, leadership, creativity and innovation, emotional intelligence, positive psychology, and neuroscience all have unprecedented consistency. We have a new level of understanding that unites an unlikely body of story, myth, belief and formal theories across business professionals, writers, mystics, academics and helpers of all kinds.

There are a set of patterns that everyone follows and choices that everyone makes that can propel us into fullest adulthood. The first pattern is that we make sense out of things until we find our safety and autonomy. Some make sense out of a very big world, and they thrive in that larger space. Some can make sense out of only a small portion of the world, so they keep to that smaller space. Some make sense in a way that is incongruent with most of us and, may be singled out for a diagnosis and treatments. Though, sometimes this incongruence is genius. Regardless of where we fall in this range, at an early point along our way we are making sense to make safety and autonomy. Some stop there.

A second pattern is that once we make sense, we work to build onto what we already have. We are reluctant to go back and shake up that foundation that we have constructed. Not only are we reluctant, we 'defend our turf'. And, we all have similar 'play books' for this defense. We choose some prophylactic combination of control, capitulation, or expertise. Some stop there.

The third pattern is that we aspire to achieve and master skills. These are inherently positive attributes, and are psychologically and emotionally rewarding. We add on to our inventory with more study, frameworks, and experience. We sometimes reach a sense of mastery and safety through our knowledge and our ability to learn. Some stop there.

The fourth pattern is that we aspire to connect with others, and all of us have a range of strategies for managing these connections. Initially, while our sense of self is not strong, we choose among three less than fulfilling connecting options:

1. One of our options is (paradoxically) to isolate ourselves. We depersonalize and objectivize another person; stranger, co-worker, and neighbor. We maintain physical, emotional and intellectual space. We tweet. We post. We text. (Ironically, these social technologies can be our way to stay impersonal). Some stop there.

2. A second option is deferring to others. We (unconsciously) assume there is no way to stand up to the fire of their person, so we comply. We defer to real (or remembered/imagined) persons such as lovers, parents, neighbors, bosses, or childhood chums. We defer to substitutes for people such as ideologies, political authority, published media, or popular images. Some stop there.

3. Finally, the third option is that we choose to dominate others. We dominate with ideas, actions, and controls. We dominate in exploiting their deference, time, confidence, and showing our superiority in effort, knowledge, materialism, or physicality. Some stop there.

Adult growth and maturity researchers have measured our adult population and find that the majority of us have stopped somewhere among some combination of the above patterns.

When we stop here we are deferring our happiness and fulfillment, abdicating it to someone or something outside of us, or confusing our fulfillment with our long-established abstractions of safety.

As a leader, the above patterns should be familiar to you. These are all part of all of our humanity. If these are not familiar to you, if you are not keenly aware of these, then you are also most likely not aware of the holds these patterns have on you. You have great and joyous learning ahead.

What would it be like if we did not 'stop there' and we kept choosing and made different choices?

"Life is a journey. When we stop, things don't go right."
~ Pope Francis

The Hunger to Be a Leader

Each of us holds a strong attraction to our own leadership and its meaning and effect on our lives, at least, a strong suspicion and intuition of this. But, in our culture, we very easily doubt ourselves and we very easily hold assumptions about leadership that sabotages our own potential. We do not have the audacity to consider our own fulfillment.

You may want to hear a one-factor strategy for growing into leadership. Instead, the strategy is multi-faceted, paradoxical, simple and complex all at once. I have included the following observations of leaders, and they may or may not be what you expect.

As you read the list, imagine yourself having these attributes. They are in who you are as well as what you do. Embrace this in your imagination.

So, here is my illustrative, but not exhaustive, list of the experience of those who embraced their authentic leadership:

- Leaders engage others. They focus outside of themselves.
- Leaders listen. They hear. They witness. They acknowledge.
- Leaders have self-awareness. They connect to their humanity and resourcefulness.
- Leaders accept personal vulnerability, as part of the cost of knowing and leading.

- Leaders intimately know their values, and a purpose that resonates with them.
- Leaders know the "why" behind what they are choosing to do.
- Leaders' constituents transform them. Leaders transform constituents.
- Leaders are self-authored, and stand in their truth.
- Leaders' whole intelligence includes intuition, emotion, instinct and rationality, knowledge, experience and the senses.
- Leaders are comfortable with the uncomfortable. Leaders relish fear and uncertainty.
- Leaders can discern the subtle distractions that show up as doubts, diversions, and saboteurs.
- Leaders hold passion for the future and obsession in their focus.
- Leaders are grounded in the here and now as the place of effective choice.
- Leaders have humble vision and bold vision.
- Leaders invite others.

A CEO of an inspirationally successful software company said to me, "Leadership happens when there is openness and inquisitiveness about possibilities, when we accept information outside of our own filters and controls, when we muster the courage to be specific in our vision, and when curiosity and passion shifts from ourselves to the story, purpose and challenges of our employees, partners and customers."

What are the Key Components of Coaching for Leadership?

In the coaching experience, you suspend your defenses and your distractions and take an honest and curious look at what you want and what is going on. You find signs and signals and information that you never realized or valued before. You give attention to stories that can be described with words like restless, hungry, stressed, annoyed, disconnected, shame, uncertain, trapped, furious and replace them with experience that has much better words.

Here is an intellectual summary of some common elements of the coaching experience:

Vision and Purpose: Finding a purpose (as you see it today) and living toward it brings insight, energy, passion and power that are propelling and contagious.

Awareness: The very process of transforming what is in your head (and heart) into words so that another person can understand is clarifying and cleansing. Similarly, the experience of being fully heard can be transforming, and is always gratifying.

Power: One of the most common expressions of satisfaction in a successful coaching relationship is about how your power emerges or intensifies, which brings a new sense of worthiness and well-being.

Challenge and Confrontation: Sometimes, we just need 'a kick in the pants,' and there is nothing like an independent view to provide it.

Authenticity, Trust and Vulnerability: Learning how to both recognize and stand in your truth is critical to living fully and to leading. Shifting your trusting and trustworthiness is nearly impossible without the participation of another person. Shifting your perceptions, thinking, behaviors and impact will probably include some courage.

Intelligence and Tools: A coach with depth in leadership performance knowledge brings a wealth of techniques, frameworks and references to help forward action and deepen your insight.

Making a Choice for Yourself or Your Team

I recently assisted in researching the personal qualities of coaches on NCAA and US Olympic Teams. A gold medal US Olympic coach's view of his purpose was to prepare the athlete as a person, in their character. At the moment of choice when they perform, it is not their skills that limit them; it is their clarity of focus on their passion over the noise of their doubts and distraction. These top athletes choose an athletic program to learn skills, but they choose a coach to learn about themselves and the self-choices that determine their success.

A family man, husband, and father recently reflected on his coaching experience. "I had not realized about needing to accept fear as a necessary part of each step that leads to my growing. It was this coaching time that caused me to realize that I'd left my own idea of passion and possibilities aside, instead of making it my point. I might have stayed in that complacency for years, maybe forever."

A client and I had a long discussion about the value of coaching. He quickly defends the value of the coaching relationship. He loves the way it challenges him and how he clarifies and shifts his awareness as a result. He readily offers that he now holds a perspective of himself and of his life, that he would not have anticipated otherwise. He is focused on rebuilding his life around what he is most passionate about, a bit scared but highly energized. I do not doubt his success for a moment.

"Each person holds so much power within themselves that needs to be let out. Sometimes they just need a little nudge, a little direction, a little support, a little coaching, and the greatest things can happen."

~ Pete Carroll

Gut Check

No matter how many studies or testimonials or arguments are made, you ultimately check your gut to see what seems true and right. Listen to your intuition, but listen well.

There is an important paradox of Leadership: if your gut senses some fear, uncertainty or doubt, then you are likely in the exact right place. These are the companions of growth and creative leadership. Your best self is not satisfied by defending safety. If you imagine leadership or personal development as only easy and comfortable, you are naïve about those things.

"Always do what you are afraid to do."
~ Ralph Waldo Emerson

Choose and Commit

Who you want to be as a leader is more subject to your choice than you may think. What you really want is up to you. If you want the exception, and not the norm, if you want the advanced version and not the past, then your best path to personal growth (as well as knowledge, experience, and connection) is with trusted partners, behind and beside you, that are engaged persistently in the mental and emotional creative space. That is the purpose of coaching.

"You can't connect the dots looking forward; you can only connect them looking backwards. So you have to trust that the dots will somehow connect in your future. You have to trust in something - your gut, destiny, life, karma, whatever. This approach has never let me down, and it has made all the difference in my life."
~ Steve Jobs

The more committed you are to living your passion, the less tolerance you have for anything that is a diversion, and the more hungry you are for attaining it. One of the rare things that you have is time and coaching is one of the quickest ways to get to where you want to go. Leaders have known this for the centuries. The term 'coach' comes directly from the 17th century term for 'the fastest way from here to there.'

Why, exactly, are you waiting? What is your choice, today?

"Know the true value of time; snatch, seize, and enjoy every moment of it. No idleness, no laziness, no procrastination, never put off till tomorrow what you can do today."
~ Philip Stanhope

99

Bottom Line

The skills that leaders use will vary with their specific role (for example, a senior executive's skills for communication vs a parent or technician's skills for communication). However, the ultimate distinction of leadership is not the technical things you can do, or your style, it is who you are.

In my own experience, and the experience that I have witnessed with my clients, there are two pivotal personal transitions that mark the distinctions of leadership. First, is the pivot to a creative stance where the leader is living in, living from, and standing authentically in the conviction of his purpose. Second, is the pivot from your own purpose and leadership (a great thing) to the purpose and leadership of others individually and collectively. These are the goals of leadership development and leadership coaching.

This leadership story may sound like naïve enthusiasm or romanticism, but it is based on the best research and science that is available. That research includes the relationships between this view of leading and performance – this is a story of results as well as personal fulfillment. You see, they go hand in hand. There is also a long list of trail-blazers who continue to tell us this same story in various ways – but our saboteur voices discount its simple power.

Leadership growth and full-person growth are more the same than they are different. The path to leading is the path to becoming someone that you know and love, and to be present in a way that enriches the leadership of others. This leadership is in everyone's reach and everyone's best interest

With appreciation.

Tom Bohinc is an expert in creative leadership and both personal and team peformance. His mission is to help each of us recognize our own leadership potential and to create an impact. Tom's passion around this has grown from over thirty years leading on the front-lines of organizations, from start-ups to global giants. He is fueled both by the energy of high-performing teams and the tragedy of under-performing ones. He has led innovations that changed industries, and witnessed too many that were not-as-successful. In all these cases the presence or absence of 'creative leadership factors' made the difference. Tom never tires of the opportunity to discover strengths in clients and their potential to thrive and to affect their world. Tom brings consulting and executive-level business experience in companies leading in their industries. He holds an MBA from The Weatherhead School at Case Western Reserve University. Tom also holds a CPCC certification as a Co-Active Coach from the esteemed Coaches Training Institute (CTI) as well as certification with The Leadership Circle. He is a member of the International Coaching Federation (ICF). He is the founder of the Auorm Group. He would love to hear from you at tom@auorm.com.

Chapter 11

Make the Connection
The Power of Vulnerability Every Man Should Know

Jeff Govoni, PCC

In the summer of 2012 I was 46, soon to be 47 and scared to death. My life up until then had gone more or less according to script—school, college, career, wife, kids—but now what? The script I was following had been presented to me almost at birth, comprised of the collective hopes and expectations of my family and the community in which I was raised. Whenever I felt confusion or noticed some anxiety over what might happen next, all I needed to do was refer to the script. It was a reliable pattern—worry, refer to script, feel assured—it gave me solace and comfort. But then one day I referred to my script and all I saw was a blank page.

> **A Personal Journey**
>
> This is my story of transition and the power of vulnerability. I'm sharing it as an offer to you to reflect on your own journey of transition. Throughout this chapter I offer you opportunities to reflect and invitations to write and share your story.

> **Tip: The First Step to Transition is Finding Your Frame**
>
> What script have you been following up until now? What role do you play in your script? How does the role you play influence how you see the world around you and the range of choice available to you? This is your frame. Knowing it is the first step to changing your frame and changing your script.

It was as if whoever had written the script had run out of interest, or time, or maybe simply thought that by the time I got to the last page, I would have run out of time. The emptiness terrified me. I felt adrift, alone and afraid, and I was ashamed to reveal my fear to others. I pulled away, first from acquaintances, then from friends, then family and eventually I pulled away even from myself. I walled myself in and rarely came out of my little existence to connect with anyone outside that wall. And so it's not without irony that in July of that year my brother invited me to see Roger Waters, the former bassist for the legendary rock band Pink Floyd, perform the entire 1979 album "*The Wall*" at Boston's Fenway Park.

It was July 12th and it was a perfect early summer night. A storm the day before had blown out to sea, taking with it the oppressive humidity that often hangs over coastal New England and leaving in its place cooler air and a breathtaking evening sky. Outside Fenway Park, the vendors on Lansdowne Street who normally sell Red Sox gear were instead selling t-shirts and posters festooned with slogans from the iconic Pink Floyd album to be performed that night. One of the more popular items for sale that evening was a plain white t-shirt with the word FEAR scrawled across in black letters on top of which lay the red circle with a slash—the international symbol for "no." NO FEAR!

When my brother made the offer to see The Wall, I received it with a mixture of excitement and trepidation. I was excited because full productions of The Wall are incredibly rare and I am a big Pink Floyd fan. My trepidation stemmed from not wanting to connect with a crowd and Roger Waters' reputation for being aloof and arrogant. In fact, the story told in The Wall is really Roger's story of isolation—a personal apology of sorts and an indictment of the institutions he blames for what ails society (schools, parents, government, and big business). Sure I wanted to see Roger Waters perform, but my mind was not in a space to hear a self-indulgent aging rock star tell me how empty my life was—I was doing a good enough job of that on my own.

But that night it was optimism, not pessimism I saw on the stage. Roger Waters was healthy and vigorous, not the brooding bully I expected. Yes, the songs were as I remembered...full of angst and

Tip:
Breaking Your Frame Starts with Embracing Vulnerability

What's just beyond the boundaries of your frame? What possibilities can
you see beyond those boundaries but just can't seem to reach?
How is the safety of your frame keeping you from breaking it?

What role is fear playing in keeping you from exploring the edges of your frame?

the language of division. Yes, their staging was as I expected...a huge
and grotesque inflatable school master terrorizing a facsimile of the
school-age Roger Waters and horrifying images of London during
the Blitz. But, instead of a deepening feeling of despair, there was
a growing sense of hope. During the performance of the title song
"The Wall," a small army of grade school students came onto the
stage all wearing that ubiquitous NO FEAR t-shirt and singing and
dancing, " . . . we don't need no education . . . Hey, teacher!

Leave those kids alone." The angry protest song had morphed
into a harmless schoolyard taunt—you silly teachers can't make us
feel less happy, less connected. When the kids came on stage, Roger (clearly happy and proud of the youngsters) introduced them as
attendees of a summer choral camp, and it was clear these kids were
having a blast. They were tan and happy and their energy was infec-
tious. As I watched them, I noticed I was crying, balling really. The
strange anonymity that comes with being in an audience gave me
permission to let down my guard, letting in the energy of those kids
and the crowd and exposing my vulnerability. It was my first sense
that something was changing in me. It was change that would take a
long time to fully mature and it would take a Dutch therapist to finally break down my wall.

Change the Story

So what changed for Roger Waters? How did he turn his story,
the story told in *"The Wall"*, a story originally of isolation and despair,
into one of turning away from fear and the power of connection?

The day after the performance at Fenway Park I was listening to the radio, and as luck would have it a station was broadcasting an interview with Roger Waters. Noticing the change in Roger Waters' outlook and appearance, the interviewer asked how the change came about. Roger acknowledged the self-limiting behavior he exhibited as a younger man and his tendency to make his world small by not trusting others.

He explained, in simple and uncomplicated language, that nothing magical had happened to him to bring about his transformation—no visitation from angels, no revelation from a near-death experience. Instead he simply noticed one day that he was tired of being in a foul mood.

> **Tip:**
> **Get Out of Your Head & Into Your Heart**
>
> Our frame, our story, and the scripts we're following all live in our head, in our minds. Most of us live our lives in our minds, puzzling through our challenges, searching for answers, ignoring our bodies. As we search for answers in our head and twist ourselves into knots we fail to notice the wisdom that resides in our bodies.
>
> Have you ever had a feeling you just can't explain? Ever just listen to your gut and ignore what your head says? Ever just listen to your heart?
>
> What your head can't see—may actually refuse to see—your body knows. What feeling are you just tired of feeling?

He was tired of feeling angry and he was tired of feeling disconnected. It was really as simple as that. The interviewer seemed to want a more nuanced story and pressed Roger a bit; there must have been more! Nope, Roger assured him, it simply was time to change.

It's human to create a story to explain how we feel. We do it without thinking. My daughter feels shame after getting a disappointing grade on her biology quiz and the teacher is dumb. My brother feels worried for his twenty-something son's job prospects and the economy is bad or his son is lazy. I feel embarrassed by a comment on my annual review and my boss just doesn't have his facts straight. Rather than simply noticing the feeling, we create a story to soothe our feelings and we add details when we notice the bad feelings need more soothing. In time, and without notice, our story is controlling us instead of us controlling it. We enroll ourselves in our own stories and we require others to enroll in them just as much as we have. We become lost in the details and we watch as the others drift away, incapable of following us down our story's complicated and convoluted path. And then one day, like Roger Waters, we realize our story has become a wall separating us from the world and from our own ability to feel.

Making the Connection

"Make the connection." That was the request (well, command really) that my Dutch tent mate, Bram de Boer made to me as he demonstrated to a group of onlookers a unique healing therapy known as haptonomy. Practiced primarily in The Netherlands, haptonomy, which derives its name from the Greek verb haptos (to touch, to attach), is the act of improving a recipient's health and well-being by making a physical connection. There is nothing sexual or creepy about haptonomy, but it does require a level of intimacy that few of us experience with anyone other than close family.

Bram and I, along with a dozen or so other travellers, were spending a week camping in Utah learning about Native American leadership traditions. Half of our group were business leaders from England, Holland, Germany and Switzerland and the other half were members of the Ojibwa tribe from Michigan's Upper Peninsula. I had earned my invitation to the journey because of a friendship and professional relationship I have with one of our Ojibwa guides. While the Native Americans all knew

> **Tip:**
> **Challenge Yourself to Push Into Discomfort**
>
> Our frame, no matter how limiting, provides us with comfort; a feeling of predictability. You may not like your frame, but at least it's familiar.
>
> In order to break our frame, in order to take that first vulnerable step, we need to embrace discomfort. It's outside our comfort zone where learning happens.
>
> How far out of your comfort zone are you willing to travel? What would be a compelling reason for you to travel outside your comfort zone?

each other, the rest of our group was total or near total strangers to one another, drawn to the journey because of our shared desire to find greater meaning in life. We were all seekers and over the course of a week in the desert we found what we were seeking—connection.

We connected in so many ways. We connected by sharing our fears—for me being with total strangers far away from the comforts of home. We connected by sharing our stories: the sales executive who worked such long hours and travelled so much that he was largely absent as his young children grew up without him; the CFO who tries not to talk much for fear of revealing his sadness over his wife's debilitating condition caused by complications in childbirth; the engineer deeply troubled by his son's struggles transitioning into adulthood. And mostly we connected by sharing ourselves by simply letting ourselves to be fully seen—human and imperfect.

We all got to see the immense power of a human-to-human connection when Bram demonstrated haptonomy. It was on the second-to-last night of our journey and Bram had built a makeshift amphitheater with a picnic table serving as the stage ringed by camp chairs. With his hand resting on my shoulder and a gentle nudge to the stage, Bram asked for a volunteer on whom he would demonstrate haptonomy. I got the message that I was to be the volunteer. What happened next was astonishing.

Before I describe what happened next it should be said that Bram and I had grown close over the past many days. Through long, directionless conversations in our tent we learned about each other's families, our successes, our failures. In early morning silent strolls, just as the sun was rising above the mesas, we became accustomed to our gates, our rhythms. In lively mealtime discussions we learned we shared an interest in classic rock and a penchant for gentle teasing. Bram and I had done the rewarding work of building a relationship based on mutual trust and respect and now Bram was going to show the gathered group the power of that relationship.

Bram motioned me to the table on which he had placed a camp mattress and asked me to lay face down with my eyes closed; much like one would for a chiropractic adjustment or a massage. Once on the table, Bram stood next to me, his hand resting firmly on my shoulder. Even though Bram and I had forged a strong relationship, he still took the time to establish an even stronger bond of trust by moving slowly and asking me simple, easy to answer questions. Bram (placing his hand on my lower back), "Do you feel my hand?" Me, "Yes." "Good. Do you feel me standing next to you?" "Yes." "Good. Can you feel the warmth of my hand?" "Yes." It went on like that for a few minutes and with each question I felt myself relax almost into a nearly hypnotic state. As he asked his question he moved around my body eventually positioning himself above me. And then, without warning, he grabbed me around my mid-section causing me to respond with an immediate startle reflex.

Truth be told, if I hadn't already established a high degree of trust with Bram, I would have been pretty freaked out and jumped off that table. But my trust in Bram was high and his response to my startle was swift. He laughed and again put his hand firmly on my lower back and simply stood there in silence for a few moments. Then he started again with the questions. "Do you feel my hand?" "Yes." Good."

With each question Bram placed more of his weight of his body onto mine. I noticed a deep warmth building between us and I could feel the thrum of Bram's breathing and heartbeat. Then Bram made his request, "Make the connection!" and maneuvering himself to the same position he was when he elicited my startle reflex, he grabbed me around my midsection—this time no startle . . . nothing. In fact, as he demonstrated to our fellow travelers, by inviting my body to make "contact" with his (a word that directly translates from Latin as "feel together"), Bram was able to move my body without any resist-

Tip:
Learning Starts With Trust

Before we can change, before we can learn and embrace our vulnerability, we must first trust in ourselves and in others. Without trust we won't take risk, with trust we can take the leap out of our frame.

What's your relationship with trust? When do you feel trust and when do you feel an absence of trust? What might change if you change your perspective regarding trust?

What relationship in your life would benefit from an infusion of trust? What change would have to happen in you in order for that trust to grow?

ance. He would tug my arm behind my back in a motion that would normally cause me pain and I barely noticed it. He could shake my normally stiff leg as if it were a string of over-cooked spaghetti. As he manipulated my tension-free body, he explained to the assembled group that he and I had joined our energies, we had made the connection and now we were sharing a deep trust.

After a minute or so of demonstrating my pliability, Bram helped me into a sitting position and stood next to me in silence, his hand again on my shoulder. After another minute, he helped me to my feet and the demonstration was over. I remember having a feeling of deep calm and comfort, the kind of feeling I have to imagine I once had when my mother or father held me in their arms. Utterly safe. Utterly comforted. Trusting in the boundless generosity that comes with love.

Failing to Notice

There is an often-cited quote by the Scottish-born psychiatrist R.D. Laing that reads more like a poem than prose:

> "The range of what we think and do
> is limited by what we fail to notice.
> And because we fail to notice
> that we fail to notice,
> there is little we can do to change;
> until we notice how failing to notice
> shapes our thoughts and deeds."

I'm no R.D. Laing scholar, but I love this quote and I choose to interpret it to serve my own purposes. For me, what we fail to notice is our feelings, not just our emotions, but more to the point the physical sensations that accompany them. Not wanting to feel the bad emotions we learn not to feel at all. We build walls to deaden the sensations, muffle the inputs coming at us from the outside world, and the more we become accustomed to being surrounded by the wall, the more we fail to notice the wall is even there. That night in the Utah desert Bram reached through my wall and made a connec-

---

Tip:
Change Starts with Noticing

The temptation to ignore the unpleasant is powerful. Like stepping over that pile of laundry your teenager refuses to pick up, we'd rather ignore what we can't accept because acceptance would require confronting reality.

What are you failing to notice? What is your blind spot? What might you be avoiding?

---

tion. The change I had started noticing that night in Fenway Park came into sharper focus that evening in the desert. Bram helped tear down my own wall.

Throughout the production of The Wall an actual wall of mammoth proportions was slowly being built on stage. Eventually the wall grows to cover the full length of the stage and totally obliterates the audience's view of the band—the connection has been broken. At the show's finale the wall is blown up, the explosion scattering debris across the stage and creating huge heaps of rubble. Once the cacophony of the wall's collapse abates, Roger Waters and the other members of his band clamber on top of a pile of debris and standing triumphant sing the final song "Outside the Wall" accompanied by a single acoustic mandolin. In the original production this song is a sort of sad dirge—a nod to the idiotic hopelessness of life, but that night at Fenway Park, owing to Roger's own transformation, the song was a hopeful hymn—a testament to our ability to overcome even the most formidable obstacles. Many months later, next to a desert creek in Utah, sitting in my camp chair, surrounded by my own band of fellow seekers and explorers, I stood on the debris of my own wall and let the feelings flow.

Jeff Govoni is founder and principal of Springtide Leadership Development. His mission is to improve the way we work and live by helping professionals of any level see with new eyes, feel with greater understanding, and discover their intrinsic capacity to lead. By helping individuals and groups notice with clarity how and who they are now, he develops their capacity to identify who and how they want to be in the future and together develops practices to get there. Jeff's approach is to guide clients through an exploration of their assessments, personal beliefs and thought patterns that drive their range of options. Through appreciative inquiry, personal reflections and practices and constructive input, Springtide Leadership clients develop the capacity to expand their range of options and chart a new course to a more desirable and effective future. Since obtaining his credential in Leadership Coaching from Georgetown University's prestigious Center for Transformational Leadership, Jeff has been working with senior leaders in the public and private sectors in Vermont, Virginia, Washington D.C., Central and South America and Canada. Jeff has worked with individuals and teams in both a coaching and in a facilitation capacity. jeffgovoni@gmail.com, www.springtideleadership.com.

Chapter 12

Let it Go
Get Ready to Stretch, Grow and Move Forward

Heidi Werther, MS, CPCC, ACC

Have you ever been challenged to establish a mantra to use as a guide for yourself? If not, what would you select if I gave you that challenge? Several years ago, I received this challenge. The mantra I selected is Let it Go. I started to embrace and continue to use Let it Go as a guide and reminder every day. When you start to become aware of what is holding you back and clarify what you want, you can start to let go, take action, and begin to move forward.

There are so many reasons people stay with "what is," the status quo. Though many people long for more or long for change, they often convince themselves that the grass isn't always greener on the other side of the fence. Thus, they choose to stay with what they know and what is comfortable, rather than risking the unknown. I've met so many people throughout my life that decided to stay put even though they weren't happy and weren't fulfilled. I've seen this in relationships, jobs, communities, religion, and more. I've done it! I've stayed in jobs that didn't offer growth or fulfillment; I've tolerated unhealthy relationships; I stayed in my familiar community because it was just that – familiar and comfortable. Why me, why others? The reasons are plentiful: fear, limiting beliefs, judgment (self and external), and comfort to name a few.

Ready for Change

What inspired you to read a book authored by several coaches with a range of focus? I'm guessing that at this juncture, you might be contemplating and exploring the next steps in your life. In my experience, people looking to work with a coach, or those who read books about coaching or authored by coaches are curious and feeling a bit stuck. They're looking to stretch, grow and move forward and seeking answers they might be having trouble finding on their own. They might be facing a transition or something similar.

As a coach, I work mostly with people in transition who are looking for that next step in their career, or looking to completely reinvent themselves. Some are evaluating their romantic relationship or have just transitioned out of a relationship and want to set themselves up for "success" in future relationships. Others are entrepreneurs facing the next step in their business challenged with limited or no experience working for a company and not having the tools to evaluate their progress. You get the picture. People looking at what's next, but not necessarily able to embrace it without some support.

This chapter will explore experiences and tips surrounding the importance of gaining clarity and self-awareness of when you are letting fear, limiting beliefs, or your negative voice keep you from going after what you want. The tips and exercises will help you to start doing what you want. Are you ready to be challenged to take action so that you can move forward and start capturing your dreams?

A Journey

Life is busy. Many of my clients describe their life as being stuck on a treadmill or running a rat race. When was the last time you stopped and just let your self be? When was the last time you paused and considered whether or not you were following your passion?

I was there, stuck on a treadmill, making excuses and holding on to limiting beliefs. I finally let myself admit I was not fulfilled in my career and recognized that this was impacting other parts of my life. I decided to stop and I gave myself permission to explore. I began working with a coach and re-discovered my innate passion of helping others. Like most people, what I was born to do – my purpose, was toyed with and interfered with throughout my life. People had expectations of me and I had expectations of myself.

As a young child, the youngest of four, I was always caring for others. I took care of our family pets. At age six, I played the role of mother's helper to my next door neighbor. At eleven years old, I began to babysit and when I was 16, I worked with disabled students in their classroom. Helping others is where I found and still find my greatest purpose. I always felt fulfilled and found meaning in these roles. When my education and thus career path positioned me to work in a corporate setting, I never felt fully alive. I wanted more of the personal one-on-one interaction in which I could truly help make a difference in people's lives. Where I did find meaning and fulfillment was in mentoring my direct reports, helping my friends facing transition or challenges, and helping my family whether it was my children, my sister, or my mom. So why wasn't I doing this in my professional life other than the mentoring? Because I followed a different path, not the path I was meant to follow. And, I felt trapped. I was afraid to let go of or veer off the path I was on.

I was fortunate. By allowing myself to explore my innate passion, my purpose, I opened myself up to choices. But first I had to let go. I had to let go of the limiting belief that if I left my job and pursued my passion, I wouldn't be as "successful" as I had been up to that point. I had to let go of the fear that I would be judged by friends, family, and co-workers. And I did – I let go. I decided to take a risk. I chose to reinvent myself in my 40s and left a job that was financially secure. I returned to school to gain the skills necessary to help others as a coach and as a mediator. I allowed myself to step out of my comfort zone and risk failing. Could I make it as a coach? Could I make it as a mediator? It was a big unknown. My friends and family believed in me and supported me, yet most people in the fields of mediation and coaching told me I couldn't make a living doing what I was meant to do. I had external voices trying to convince me this wasn't a good move and my own internal negative voice challenging me every step of the way. I had to learn to recognize this voice and push it aside and let my inner authority, my positive voice, take control. The negative voice or inner critic always comes back, and the awareness that I now have of how this voice can hold me back, in fact, helps me to persevere.

TIP

Start to recognize your negative voice – your inner critic.
Hints include words like can't, should, need.
When you become aware of your negative voice
try to push it aside or control it.
Your inner authority or your positive voice knows what you truly want.
Pay close attention…ask yourself, what do I want?
Follow your inner authority!

Learning from Children

What if you were able to discover, or re-discover, the person you were meant to be? What if instead of allowing fear, self-doubt, limiting beliefs, or other's expectations of you get in your way, you let them go and allowed yourself to take risks without worrying about failing or making a mistake? Imagine opening yourself up to being curious.

Have you ever watched a child learn how to crawl, to walk, to talk? They make mistake after mistake. They fall down and they get back up again, continuing to try until they figure it out. They don't worry about what has happened. Without taking the risks they do, they would never progress. Without being curious, they would not grow, stretch and develop.

CONSIDER

What lessons can you take from young children and apply to your own desires or needs to grow, stretch, develop and move forward?
Write down your thoughts.

Connection:

Pick up a journal or paper that you can return to at a later time and complete the following exercises:

- Name one dream that you have.
  - Are you following your dream?
    - If not, what's stopping you?

- Think of a time, any time in your life, when you took a risk and you advanced, you grew, you developed.
  - Where were you?
  - What was the experience like?
  - What can you take from this experience to help you take a new risk in order to stretch yourself and move forward?

- What is something you have been putting off?
  - Name it. By acknowledging it, you can start to take action.
  - What do you notice about your "reason" to avoid or procrastinate?
  - What are you aware of?
  - Is this a small task, or something that is larger and might require breaking down into smaller steps in order to tackle it?

Time to Take Action

After reviewing the stories below, I encourage you to make a commitment to yourself to complete the exercises that follow. You get to decide on the order in which to complete the exercises and you get to determine the timing. These exercises will provide you with the opportunity to start letting go, face your fears, allow yourself to be vulnerable, take risks, be curious, and have fun while you stretch, grow, and move forward.

Challenge yourself – take a bold action.

Consider acknowledging one of your fears and addressing it.

Below are two examples that I hope inspire you.

A few years ago I was challenged to climb a 40 foot tree up to a platform. Following the climb, I had to rappel from this platform. Even though this was a safe exercise, I was terrified. I was secured by a harness with ropes and the ropes were anchored by people on the ground so that I would not fall. I had never experienced anything like this. By allowing myself to put my trust in others, something I had never been good at, and take the risk that they would have my back, I let go of my fears and jumped. It was an exhilarating challenge and I loved it!

What this taught me was that by letting go, in this instance, by letting go of my inability to trust and by facing my fear, I was able to experience something new, something exhilarating, something that allowed me to stretch, grow and see new possibilities. This experience enhanced my awareness helping me to realize that I wanted more, more of these exhilarating challenges and more from life.

Another example is portrayed by my client Janet who was a "creature of habit." Janet consistently stayed within her comfort zone. For instance, when she went to her class at the gym, she stood in the same place every time. To step outside of her comfort zone, she challenged herself to move to a different spot and noticed she was experiencing her class from a different perspective. She liked it. She noticed she started working out harder and realized she had been holding herself back from the true challenge of a great workout. As she moved about the room, she continued to see things from a different view, and she reported that with each change, she was stretching, achieving greater results and was more fulfilled. Janet experimented with her running as well. Always a treadmill runner, she decided to try running outdoors. She didn't realize she had reached a plateau on the treadmill, and by running outdoors and changing up her route, she found new energy, started running further distances, and overall felt ignited by the scenery.

Step Out of Your Comfort Zone

⇨   Consider something you can do that will take you out of your comfort zone; something that will help you to let go, stretch, grow, and see new possibilities.

- Write it down.
- Write down by when you will accomplish this task, exercise or activity.
- Write down who you will tell, how you will tell them and by when.
- Next, take action!
- Notice what it was like.
- What did you discover?

Ask for Help

Many people are afraid to ask for help for fear of showing their vulnerability; fear of being judged; fear of being seen as incapable or less than "perfect"; fear of rejection. The reality is that we learn by asking questions, by asking for help…and people like to help.

One of my clients was quite curious and wanted to grow in her career, yet she was also concerned she would risk her credibility in her job if she admitted she needed help. She believed that everyone else in her company had the answers. In challenging her to show her vulnerability and ask for help, she came back to me and told me, "I learned I am too hesitant, too nervous. I don't always have the answer and I thought everyone else had the answers. I learned that everyone was trying to figure out the answers and by opening up; we [my colleagues and I] were able to work collaboratively to try to figure it out together. The takeaway lesson is that I will be bold and ask more questions and I will be bold by making decisions. I will let go of my fear of being judged."

Open Yourself Up to Being Vulnerable

⇨   Choose something you need help with.

- Ask a colleague, friend or partner for help with that issue or action.

119

- Notice how he or she reacts.
- Notice what happens for you when you ask for help.
- Journal about the experience.
- What did you learn?
- How was this helpful?

Learn Something New

Sometimes we avoid trying something new for fear we will fail, or we won't be "good enough." When was the last time you learned something new? I'm not necessarily talking about reading and gaining new knowledge, but rather a task, a hobby, something that could challenge you physically, emotionally or intellectually?

Working with my client Trish, she accepted a challenge to pick up a new hobby or activity that would help her to slow down, relax, and pull her away from her habit of overworking or constantly finding chores to occupy her time. She reflected on the fact that her mom loved to work with her hands and was always in awe of her mother's talent. Trish was convinced she, herself, had no artistic talent. So I challenged her to try something she had either never tried before, or hadn't tried in a long time so she could learn a new skill or craft and let go of her limiting belief that she didn't have what it took. She decided she wanted to learn how to knit so that she wasn't just doing something, but she would actually be creating something. She was a bit ambivalent as she said she tried knitting when she was younger, and it never turned out right. She had for so long avoided taking up a creative hobby for fear she would fail or be judged on the outcome. What she discovered is that she hadn't been giving herself permission to slow down and enjoy life. By taking up knitting, she felt empowered to let go of her old habits of overworking and "overdoing."

Ready To Learn!

⇨ Think about something you have wanted to learn but have been avoiding.

- Write down a few reasons why you might have been avoiding this.

- Set a date to start learning. Write it down.
- Commit to sticking it out until you have learned the task, craft, skill or activity.
- When you start the learning process, pay attention to your reactions.
- Write down what you notice.
- Pay close attention to your attitude.
- Notice how your body reacts.
- Is your negative voice trying to dissuade you in any way?
- Are you excited that you are learning something new or maybe frustrated with the process?
- How do you feel when you complete the learning process?
- What possibilities have opened for you?
- Celebrate your accomplishment!

Congratulations!

Imagine the possibilities. I'm so excited for you and hope you thoroughly enjoy or have already enjoyed the exercises. Celebrate each completion! You are on your way to Embracing Positive Change. Boldly let go of what's holding you back. Have fun being curious and delight in the risks you start to take. Reframe - consider mistakes as opportunities for learning, for growth, for development and for moving forward.

Passionate about empowering others in transition, certified professional coach, mediator, facilitator and consultant, Heidi Werther works with individuals, families and organizations in transition inspiring them to embrace changes that fuel constructive results. Her 25 years in the business world, along with her personal experiences, defined her coaching niche working with individuals looking for the next step in their career or looking to completely reinvent themselves; entrepreneurs or small business owners requiring a guide as they define or expand their business; people looking for more in their relationships and parents looking to improve their co-parenting skills. An expert in her field through her work achievements, academic studies, and personal life experiences, Heidi listens to her clients, helps them to clarify their purpose, communicate their dreams, desires and goals, and challenges them to take action allowing them to move forward in the direction they choose. She believes her clients have the answers within. Heidi obtained her Master of Science, Mediation and Applied Conflict Studies from Champlain College, and her coaching certification, Certified Professional Co-active Coach (CPCC), from the highly acclaimed Coaches Training Institute (CTI). She is an active member of the International Coaching Federation (ICF) and its New England Chapter, as well as several mediation associations and facilitator's groups. Heidi is the proud parent of two wonderful young men who opened her eyes to curiosity, the true meaning of passion, and the benefits of taking risks. Heidi Werther, MS, CPCC, ACC, 617.365.9550, heidiwerther.com.

Chapter 13

Change...
A Journey of Hope and Healing

Jeanne C. Zuzel, RN, MA

"Do not go where the path may lead, go instead where there is no path and leave a trail."
                                    ~ Ralph Waldo Emerson ~

C hange is inevitable and happens with every breath we take. How we as humans react to change is what often stirs up our "stuff." I work with clients everyday who desire to make changes in their lives or who are reacting to changes that have occurred.

Change is different for everyone. I think about change in two ways, change of choice and change of occurrences. Change of choice addresses the changes we choose to make. Change of occurrences happens when "things" happen beyond our control that creates a sudden change. The one factor that remains the same is our need for support. I ask my clients to remember that change is a process and not an event. It is the most complex phenomenon we experience in our life journey, and it is change that makes our journey possible. The decision to make or accept a change in our life is often thought of as "impossible or far reaching." Let's shift that thinking just a bit. Allow yourself to envision making a change as a long WALK to a distant place...New England to California perhaps. Think about this trip as your journey through the change that has occurred or the changes you would like to create.

What has occurred that has set you on this journey to begin with? Is it a life changing event like a birth, death, or divorce? Have you decided to make a significant change like losing weight, moving, or going back to school? No clue where to begin?

My Journey

Change occurred for me as a series of life events. This set me on my journey of hope and healing. My beautiful 14-year-old daughter decided she no longer wanted to live. She attempted to fulfill her decision three times in one year and was admitted to a residential care facility 100 miles away from our home. My son, then a senior in high school, was leaving for college and struggled through issues of separation and independence. My husband, a kind and gentle man who I have the honor of being married to for 36 years was in the throws of indecision, turmoil, and inconsistency in his job of 18 years.

My journey led me to discover that similar to most women I knew, I lived for my family. My need was to "fix" everything, or make certain there was never a need to "fix" something. Yes. I was a control freak! If they gave out a PhD in control, I had earned it, or so I thought. My family in crisis became my "Wake Up' call. It was loud and clear. A voice deep inside said, "Until you look at yourself and your life, nothing will ever be enough." I saw myself as a professional, confident, woman, mother, nurse and suddenly I realized I was living for others and about others. I was convinced it was my job to be who others thought I was. I was angry and often resented the opinion of others, but I had convinced myself it must be true. I went out of my way to please the "others" at the expense of my true self, health and wellbeing. I know for many of you this is a familiar scenario.

When I began my journey, I was 60 lbs overweight, didn't sleep well, never exercised and was described by most people as "angry and controlling." I did feel angry, and I knew I was better than that and that I deserved peace of mind, body and spirit. I sought the help of a very skilled therapist, who also practiced a gentle and consistent body centered energy therapy. I was able to make my journey to self-love, self-respect and self-care. The journey I took was a change of choice, one of self-love, self-commitment and healing. I walked this journey one step at a time, one minute at a time, one hour at a time, and one day at a time. With my eyes directed in front of me, I always moved forward. There were times on the journey, however, that I proceeded so slowly that it seemed as if I was at a stand still or perhaps back tracking. Often the path was steep and rocky. The forests were so thick with vegetation that it was hard to see where I was going. I could not "see the forest for the trees." It is at those times that I remembered that I was never alone and could always ask for help. With determination, help and support, I was able to navigate a clear path once again and could actually pick up speed. The valleys I encountered gave me respite, time to rejuvenate, recharge and prepare for the next set of hills and forests I encountered. It was hard and joyous and filled with unexpected adventure and in the end…worth every step I took.

Beginning Your Journey – Change of Choice

I often tell my clients that every journey needs a period of preparation before we begin. This is the time we take to sort out where we think we want to go, who we need to take with us or ask for help from, and what "supplies" will help us to get there. Do not concern yourself with the hows, whys, and what ifs…this only allows judgment and fear to cloud your vision. Keep your vision clear and going forward.

The following is a list of basic "supplies" that may be beneficial:

- A map: an idea of what change you are trying to make
- A good pair of walking shoes: support for the road ahead
- A walking stick: someone to lean on when the terrain gets rough
- An umbrella: shielding from the elements
- Sunglasses: opportunity to lessen the glare and keep your eyes wide open
- Clothing in layers: to be able to adjust when the temperature or climate shifts

The Map

Let's start with the map. This contains the change you want to make and your path to get there. Remember that the journey is never a straight line and we must always take into consideration the topography of the environment we are traveling through. Creating changes in your lifestyle may reveal that the topography may contain a few hills, rocks, streams, lakes or oceans that need to be navigated in order to go forward. You may need to engage in crucial communications with others to smooth out the terrain. Perhaps you need to set some new boundaries and this will cause some waves to form. Do you need to rebuild a bridge that was once demolished? Or get some help to build a raft to keep you afloat?

When beginning a journey of change of choice, it is helpful to let people know what you are doing, especially your close friends and family. This allows you to obtain support and also lets others know they are in for a change as well. Any change we create has a ripple effect on the people around us and they may not be willing to go with the new flow. It is kind and courteous to include others that will be affected by your changes.

When I no longer made every decision for my college-aged son, he revolted and refers to this as the time when his mother "dropped him." He was so accustomed to having me solve all of his problems that he felt abandoned and ill-equipped to do it on his own. The truth was he was perfectly capable and has continued to be self reliant and easily navigates his own path.

Our journey is often met with obstacles and we must be prepared to handle them or rest in order to gain the strength to handle them. Unless your map is current, you will find that some roads are no longer open and many freeways have barriers or construction that must be considered along the way. This concept suggests that if you are living in the past it will become clear very quickly that your continued focus on the past no longer serves you if your desire is to move forward. Allowing your energy to be focused on past hurts, events and issues will keep you stuck in traffic forever.

Walking Shoes

A good pair of shoes gives your feet wonderful support and protection from the elements. What kind of support will you need on your journey to create the change you desire in your life? Perhaps you are the flip-flop/sandal type that lets the sand flow through your toes. This is great for the beach, but not so good when you reach a snow storm or hurricane. Maybe you prefer hiking boots. They offer great strength and protection and they serve you well in forests, rocks and hills, but aren't really helpful or necessary on the beach or swimming across a river. It's important to start with something stable and be open to adding additional shoes based on the conditions you encounter.

Walking Stick

A good stable shoe may be your desire to change and your walking stick is your support. Support may be a professional Health & Wellness Coach that you have interviewed and chosen to walk with you as you create changes in your lifestyle. It is important to have someone to lean on. Your walking stick needs to be strong and sturdy with a non-slip tip. A good friend can serve this purpose, and often that is a great way to begin. Be open to adding a professional "hiker" should the need arise. I begin all my "walking stick" relationships by offering the client a journal. It is a tool for them to express their needs, hopes, fears, and dreams. It can be the best friend that always listens or the list of to do's that they are in need of. A journal is personal and available whenever you need it. It can show progress and remind us of how we have weathered each storm.

The Umbrella

It is not unusual for storms to blow up when we are trying to make significant changes in our life. A good storm can actually be the catalyst that brings about the need for change. Storms in our life journey are very similar to actual weather. These storms can range from a mild rain, where a simple umbrella can serve as good protection, to a raging hurricane/tornado/snow storm. When the elements are too strong for the equipment we have, that's when we need to seek shelter from the storm and often just wait it out. How will you wait out the storms that will come as part of your journey?

Storms have several purposes:

1. They force us to go inside; seeking shelter and self-discovery.
2. They require provisions for the future; in case we lose power what do we need?
3. They force togetherness; communication with each other is essential to survival.
4. They can clear anything that is not secured; if it's not there when the storm is over, did you really need it?

When the storm clears we often have a new or different perspective.

Sunglasses

The discovery process can shine a light on a previously dark area of our lives. This light can be blinding if we rip the shade back too quickly and can lead us to retreat back into the darkness. A good pair of sunglasses can serve you well. They will protect you from sudden bursts of light and offer protection in the wind. Courage is your pair of sunglasses. Courage allows you to consider each burst of light for the illumination it sheds and the healing that it can offer you. Remember that you can put your glasses on and shield the light for a while until your eyes get used to the new perspective you have discovered. Heading into blinding light can lead you off the path of your journey and you may end up on a different road. This too is part of the journey, learning to navigate back to where you decided you were going or finding out that there are many ways to "get there." I know that when I decided to change my body weight, I got off the path many times until I finally learned how to use the sunglasses to my advantage and keep on going. I changed paths a lot until I found one that felt good to me. I welcomed the light, my discovery, the blind spots, the bumps in the road and kept on going.

Layers of Clothing

The journey from one place to another requires consideration of climate changes as well as terrain. Parts of your journey can feel hot and uncomfortable. What will you need to cool down? Do you have enough layers to weather the cold? And what if you need to shed everything to swim and start again once you reach the other side of the river? We can never anticipate all of our needs. Protection from the "elements" comes in a variety of ways. Layers of protection are needed in parts of our journey, and we need to be prepared to shed those layers as soon as possible when we realize we no longer need them. Connection and conversation can assist us in determining how quickly the layers can be shed.

Some of us protect ourselves with physical, spiritual and emotional distance. Our life journey will continue to gain ground with connection and conversation. It is through connection and conversation that we can come to resolution and move forward toward change. What conversations do you need to have?

It is interesting that protection from the extremes of weather requires the same action as dealing with our emotional extremes. When you are really angry and "hot" we want to shed our anger, and often we do…at others. When we are depressed and lonely life can appear dark and cold and we cover up, often adding more layers.

Recognizing our reactions can assist us with creating new actions. Action fuels our change process as much as respite. The healing journey is a series of resting and moving forward.

Change is inevitable. It is a process and not an event. Gather support; accept encouragement and have patience and it can be a welcome process. I congratulate you for your curiosity and courage and invite you to begin your journey of hope and healing through change.

Jeanne is owner and Clinical Director at INCITE Wellness Center in Norwich CT. She is a pioneer in Holistic Health Care and has a private Integrated Therapy/ Lifestyle Medicine practice. Jeanne is a Registered Nurse of 38 years. She combines her clinical expertise and nursing experience with practical application of Integrative Health and Wellness concepts. Jeanne believes that change is a process and NOT an event… She supports her clients through all phases of the change process. *This invites her clients and students to experience the opportunity for ultimate personal growth, learning and healing. Jeanne is an Adjunct Professor at local colleges and enhances her practice by offering sessions and seminars in Healing Touch, Expressive Art, Holistic Health, Wellness and Stress management. Jeanne is a Certified Healing Touch Practitioner and Instructor. She has a Master's degree in Integrative Health and Healing, a Certificate in Expressive art therapy and is a board certified Nurse Health & Wellness Coach. Jeanne is available to support your journey. You may contact her via email : incite.learn@ yahoo.com, or telephone 860-889-4690. Visit her website : www.newincites.com.*

Chapter 14

Tending to Our Inner World to Create Better Results in Our Outer World

Lynnea Brinkerhoff, MSOD, PCC

It is said in Buddhism that the nature of life is suffering...
The key is to not suffer over your suffering!

What's the Larger Problem and Why 21st Century Skillsets are Needed?

We live our lives surrounded by external realities that affect our sense of well-being. Be it the effects of globalization, the constant threat of environmental degradation or an experience of economic loss, we live in an increasingly impersonal world that places ever more demand on us. The current economy provides only temporary satisfaction, mostly in the form of a quick fix that distracts us from the things that could bring lasting satisfaction. Too often, we miss the nuances that make life meaningful amidst the stress of our busy lives. Do we experience sanity and coherence in our life and our work or do we feel alienated from ourselves?

Do We Experience a Sense of Being at Home in the World?

I believe we are accumulators - of stuff, concepts, toxins, habits, mindsets and rules. This accumulation is the primary reason for unhealthy stress in the body, mind and spirit. Families, organizations and communities are the same way. They become repositories for outdated patterns of behavior, otherwise known as 'bad habits' or dysfunctional behavior. It is our duty to find creative ways to clean our vessel. We are invited to become a 'self-cleaning oven' and learn to act from a beginners mind. It is a moment to moment discipline. When we do not have a spiritual or a physical practice, whether it's breathing, walking, praying or something else, then we become tense, less healthy and lose touch with our best self and our capacity for effective action in short order!

21st Century Survival Formula:

$$E = P - I$$
(Excellence = Performance − Interference)
What are your main interferences?
What depletes you? What gives you energy?
…Do what gives you energy

The demands of contemporary life call for 21st Century Skills that encourage us to make the right choice about:

- Which conversation do we want to be in?
- What are we saying yes or no to?
- Who we spend our time with that fuels our inner fire and stimulates our best?
- How much do we choose the digital life or the natural world?
- How much stress is good for us and when does anxiety cripple us?

Whether it's the end of a love affair or we are starting a new job or if we cannot find our keys, we are likely to respond with our particular flavor of anxiety. Much of this is determined by how those we looked up to early in life handled their stress. Most of us lack the awareness that we have a wide variety of responses available to us when confronted with conflicting priorities, the threat of loss or even the potential of a big success. Whether we deem things good or bad, change today is constant and with change comes tension or stress. The question we must confront is how do we handle stress skillfully and when does stress get the better of us?

Research shows that we need ample tension in order to be productive in the world. Just enough tension on a bicycle wheel, for instance, keeps it moving forward and not collapsing to the side. Just enough tension allows you to be in what author Mihaly Csikszent-

> **We adapt and change only when**:
> It is **logical** -
> Does it make sense to me?
> It is **feasible** -
> Do I have the resources to do it?

mihalyi calls the 'sweet spot for learning' in his book called "*Flow*," a state in which you are neither bored nor overwhelmed.

Case Study: Wendy, a senior female executive in the medical industry needed a different kind of coaching. Wendy did not find the corporate coaches that her company had prescribed for all these years helpful. She needed to go beyond the assessments, checklists and the standard line about turning her performance around in 90 days. She wanted to:

- ⇨ get beyond her usual defenses,
- ⇨ be approached with both clarity and care,
- ⇨ observe and understand her own behavior,
- ⇨ develop strategies for trying out new solutions,
- ⇨ build self-regard and accept her shortcomings,
- ⇨ become a leader and a partner she could be proud of and others could be inspired by.

She reached out after being told that she scared the people around her. They said she was judgmental, harsh and dismissive when giving feedback. She did not help people develop. Wendy was not accustomed to falling below her expectations and she had no tools to deal with that reality either internally (emotionally) or externally (practically). She was depressed and found herself going through the motions rather than living with gusto. She was lonely and found it hard to trust others.

Wendy began to realize that, while she excelled at the technical or 'hard' skills of being a manager, she did not enjoy the key relationship skills that are vital for success. She needed to see that the **'soft'** skills are actually what Dr. John Scherer calls the **'tough stuff'**. She needed to learn to reframe her life and her frustrations in a larger context.

The following questions helped Wendy begin to see things differently.

⇨ What would a full and engaging life look and feel like?
⇨ What is happening just before you feel you are going to lose it or say something you regret?
⇨ What needs do you legitimately have and how can you communicate them gracefully?
⇨ What kinds of things give you energy and what takes your energy away?
⇨ What are some strategies you could use to get yourself back on track when you lose it?
⇨ How can you create more sustainable relationships, with loved ones, colleagues, bosses and employees?

Wendy began to step out in new ways, to rebuild quality relationships and to receive a recognition she never imagined possible. She was singled out as one of the top 14 global women leaders in her company and was selected for a special leadership development program. Funny thing, results show up outside, in 'the world' when we have the courage to complete the 'inside job' of building our emotional intelligence and resilience to develop the soft skills that make the difference. Challenges as well as breakthroughs seem to fall into two main categories: inner satisfaction and outer results. In this case, Wendy saw improvements in both and her life made more sense in the process.

> A good coach should be able to serve like the bumpers in a bowling alley – the banks that rise up on the sides to ensure you don't fall into the ditch on the left or right.

It is said that people want to read a story or hear a talk on the chance that they can be one who gets the lesson without having to experience the hardship. This is illustrated by a favorite quote from *"The Art of War"* by Lao Tse:

"Learn to sweat on the sidelines so you don't have to bleed on the battlefield."

How I Came to See that Our Clients Need What I Needed: Radical Nourishment

I was an outdoor leadership guide, spent time in hospitality and media sales. I traveled twice around the world and have been coaching since the late 80's. I am an educator and author of organization development. I found a natural role as counsel to those with the power to affect changes that are driven by a 'positive dissatisfaction with the status quo'.

By studying the world's wisdom traditions, I gained greater fluency to relate to many types of people. It also led me back to my love of nature and to further hone my understanding of what it means to develop the whole person. The real breakthrough came when I had enough difficult and obvious failures. I went out on too many limbs and became cocky about what I thought I knew. I did not care for myself effectively and ended up traumatized, bankrupt and betrayed.

I was flat on all counts and had nothing to look forward to or build upon. I had lost focus on my professional life to dedicate my energies to saving the environment, but did not consider a strategy to simultaneously take care of myself. Each of my edgy, forward thinking undertakings tanked. I needed to go deep inside to restore myself.

I began to ask my clients the same question that lifted me out of the hole I had been stuck in.

If you were dropped in the middle of a remote village, how would you serve with your head, hand and heart? I learned to help in the arenas of wellness and collaboration, deepening people's relationships with nature, themselves and each other. I saw my life more as a journey and less as aimed at a destination. Everything became a form of a vision quest.

135

When we stand at a crossroads, three questions can help guide us:

Do we choose to step over the threshold and embrace the change that has already happened?

Can we see what is no longer accurate about who we are?

Are we willing to lay down the arms that have protected us for a lifetime and pick up the next phase of our life?

For me, I looked at what I was good at and what the world needed. I realized that I had to champion my own human journey, not pathologize or make myself guilty over what has not worked. Rather, I needed to see the perfection of what happened, drop underneath my at times crippling anxiety and develop the freedom to choose the right next step.

It is possible today to die and live multiple lives inside of this one precious life. We need to learn to move from stressed to blessed by offering ourselves and each other a form of radical nourishment through surrounding ourselves with that which regenerates us, not tears us down. I came to knowing that I wanted to serve the whole person in a deeper way than I had up to that time and still maintain legitimacy and income in my work in the corporate world. I strengthened my emotional, physical and spiritual resilience and forged a path that moved beyond the either/or and integrated both of my aspirations that led me to understand how much my corporate clients were in search of Radical Nourishment™.

As the famed poem of 1927, written by Max Erhmann, The Desiderata aptly states:

> Take kindly the counsel of the years, gracefully
> surrendering the things of youth.
> Nurture strength of spirit to shield you in sudden misfortune.
> But do not distress yourself with dark imaginings
> Many fears are born of fatigue and loneliness.

Radical Nourishment™ - RN for the Soul

Rad-i-cal: of or going to the root or origin; fundamental; going to extreme, especially as regards change from accepted or traditional forms; forming a basis or foundation.

Nour-ish-ment: sustenance; the act of nourishing or being nourished.

RN for the soul means surrounding yourself with all the ingredients that have you feeling well-fed, crafting a life that fits for who you are and one that gives back to you when you stop trying to live it. It's about feeling at home in the world, in your skin and being willing to dwell, sometimes uncomfortably, in your inner world to receive greater results in the outer world. Applying self-soothing techniques in times of mini and major crises and being willing to 'get off the ledge and back on your edge' (from The Stress Squad) are hallmarks that you are living a life that is radically nourishing.

Physical Health:
Full function
Energy
Comfort/Sense of wellbeing

Emotional Health:
Full range of emotions
Loving relationships
Ample joy

Mental Health:
Able to solve problems
Clear focus
Both logical and creative thinking

Spiritual Health:
Sense of meaning & purpose
Inner peace
Sense of connection to your Source

Therefore, as your coach in this moment…I am inviting you to a life of radical nourishment, in which you mindfully depart from your norm by fanning the embers of your inherent strengths and aspirations such that you become fully engaged with your life and others are sustained and nourished by what you do.

Resilience

Everyone has a natural capacity to 'bounce back' from minor shocks and to move forward in the face of challenge. Animals literally 'shake off' their traumas and begin again (or go back to grazing). We call this capacity 'resilience'. Over time, our natural capacity can get clogged and needs to be refreshed.

Resilience Muscles You Can Build Right Now

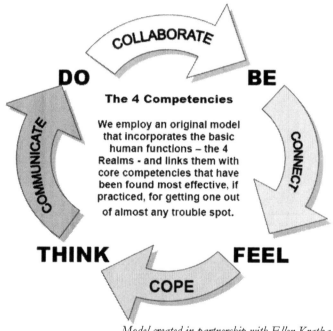

The 4 Competencies

We employ an original model that incorporates the basic human functions – the 4 Realms - and links them with core competencies that have been found most effective, if practiced, for getting one out of almost any trouble spot.

Model created in partnership with Ellen Kratka

1) BE: Can you connect with your experience right now?

It is important to be aware of sympathetic -vs- parasympathetic nervous system responses: Are you anxiety driven or aspiration-driven? Anxiety draws forth adrenaline which can give you energy in the short run and cause premature aging and adrenal exhaustion in the long run. Shortness of breath, sweaty hands, and tight muscles are all symptoms indicating that your sympathetic nervous system has kicked into overdrive. Endorphins are more subtle and bring a gradual and more sustainable sense of well-being. Sipping water or exhaling or looking at something beautiful for 30 seconds while you take a full breath can bring you back on line. Organs function better and so does overall health. Do everything you can to keep your parasympathetic nervous system running the show.

2. FEEL: Can you cope with the changes that are coming your way or do you need a break?

"Stress enhances function (physical or mental, such as through strength training or challenging work) and may be considered positive. Persistent stress that is not resolved through coping or adaptation, deemed distress, may lead to anxiety or withdrawal (depression) behavior. The difference between experiences is determined by the disparity between an experience (real or imagined), personal expectations, and resources to cope with the stress. Alarming experiences, either real or imagined, can trigger a stress response."

~ Hans Selye

What is your stress limit and how much stress can you tolerate and still perform well?

- **Are you in the Green where everything is sailing along?**
- **Are you in the Yellow where you have lots of warning signs that you are about to implode or explode?**
- **Are you in the Red already over your edge.**

No matter what your work, think of your new job description as staying in the green and the yellow.

3) THINK: Can you communicate what you are feeling and what you need?

If we don't get these needs met we grow irritable and either act out (explode) or withdraw (implode). So until we know that we have them, how do we know to meet them?

⇨ Safety and security
⇨ Fun and play
⇨ Variety
⇨ Love and affection
⇨ Boundaries
⇨ Sleep
⇨ Contribution

4) DO: Can you step out onto the playing field and collaborate with others?

Let yourself be radically nourished by a coach who should be able to offer the following:

⇨ **Build Rapport**: Gentle easing in and meeting you where you are;
⇨ **Create the Contract**: Gain clarity about what you want and your readiness to have it;
⇨ **Observe and Inquire**: Mine your various perspectives to see how they serve you given your mission; offer ample feedback, both constructive and appreciative;
⇨ **Recognize opportunity**: Listen to your spoken and unspoken aspirations; sense the emerging opportunities;
⇨ **Embody the future**: Scenario plan with your hardest and most desired scenario in mind; run post play reviews and relieve you as you prepare to take 'guiltless retry's';
⇨ **Support your plan**: Partner with you to build certain muscle groups, hone your vision, attract what you want and become more of who you are meant to be.

> **Seek comfort when you are too challenged and challenge when you are too comfortable.**

Questions for Self-coaching: (or have a friend ask these of you…take your time)

❖ What's important to you and how is this situation right for you?

❖ What would you rather be seeing/feeling/doing/having?

❖ What have you tried already and what support have you gotten or not?

❖ What is most in your way from having what you want?

❖ Are there any relationships or organizations that could help you get what you want that you have not been willing to reach out to?

❖ What would you be willing or not willing to do to have what you say you want?

❖ If it's working the way that you really want it to, what would be happening in your life? How would you feel? And if it doesn't happen for you, then what?

❖ What one action can you take to move the ball down the field…right now?

Conclusion

Once we have received adequate support and mirroring in the form of Radical Nourishment™, we can begin to coach ourselves. It is vital in the process of development to have someone else be our witness and our guide. A coach has the rare privilege to join with another's inner world and see the constructs by which they behave, bringing them clearly into the light.

You can learn to keep the tension at just the right level, to use humor, to give yourself virtual hugs, to be both direct and compassionate and to ask the questions you would not usually ask yourself.

Then you will invite yourself to step over the proverbial threshold at the exact moment when you are ready for it. You will learn to build your capacity to become comfortable with discomfort and to come home to yourself...again and again.

Lynnea Brinkerhoff, founder of Radical Nourishment™, is a Board Certified Executive and Wellness Coach, International Coach Federation PCC level and Board member. She brings 25 years of experience in operational and strategic roles in hospitality, healthcare and wilderness-based education to her work with leaders in transition who are seeking greater results, satisfaction and resilience in life and purpose-driven work. Co-founder of the StressSquad™ and the first Eco-therapy program on the east coast, Lynnea is a seasoned practitioner of several integrative health methods and continues to seek remedies for modern day maladies. She also serves as Disaster Chaplain for NYC. She has authored works in resilience, neuroscience of leadership, organizational alignment, equine assisted coaching and collaborative strategic planning. Lynnea has an ability to put people at ease, to sense into their unspoken aspirations and fears and, using a strengths-based, no-nonsense approach, turning them into concrete operational results. Lynnea invites people to see their repeating patterns, the needs of their stakeholders and to choose the most effective path forward to accomplish their mission. She enjoys cayenne pepper and swims in the ocean on New Year's Day for the last 25 years. www.Lynneabrinkerhoff.com, www.EponaDevi.com, www. TriStateSoulfulCeremonies.com, Lynneabrink@gmail.com.

Epilogue

Now what? That's the question I kept asking myself when I finally decided to leave a job I absolutely loved because I was working for a company with a completely chaotic and volatile management team. I was totally lost. I found myself wandering around a bookstore one day and happened upon a book called "Now What?: 90 Days to a New Life Direction," by Laura Berman Fortgang. Considering that's the exact question I was asking myself, it's no surprise I immediately bought the book.

In this book, pioneering life coach Laura Berman Fortgang shared the process that she used successfully to help hundreds of clients make major changes in their lives. The book provided a clear and infinitely practical 90-day program and access to your own personal life coach. Life coach? I'd heard of coaching before, but thought of it in terms of athletes and sports teams. I didn't even know a career like that existed. Over the next 3 months, I was amazed by the progress and transformation that occurred in my life as a result of working with a coach. So amazed in fact, that I decided to pursue a life coaching certification. I can honestly say it was one the best things I've ever done in my life. The personal development, transformation and listening skills I learned changed me in ways I would never have imagined. I truly believe that everyone can benefit from enrolling in a life coaching program or working with a life coach. To this day, I still work with life and business coaches and I wouldn't give them up for anything. They've helped me grow businesses, know when to stay and when to get out of relationships, realize my true purpose, and talked me off many ledges! I owe most of my success to the work I've done with these amazing people.

Until we know our true purpose for being here, many of us wander aimlessly from one job to the next or one relationship to the next, always searching for something that will make us happy. The great spiritual masters teach that we will never find happiness by looking for it outside of ourselves. To be truly fulfilled or enlightened as they say, we must find peace within our own mind and body. To find peace you have to truly know yourself, what your soul wants, what your ego wants, as both play an important role in finding your purpose and living your dreams. Your soul will give you clues as to what your purpose is, while your ego will put you in action on obtaining your goals and desires. We need to respect the needs of both in order for the process to work.

Before taking steps towards finding your purpose you may need to do some self-development work and meditation. Here's where having a coach is absolutely essential. It is important to find a coach that is certified through an International Coach Federation (ICF) accredited coach training program and one that is the right fit for you. A good coach will partner with you in forming a clear vision of what you want in your life, brainstorm new ideas or solutions to get you there, and will keep you on track and moving forward to reach your goals and dreams.

Because of the impact life coaching has had on my life, I was guided and inspired to create the vision for this book you're holding in your hands. A collaboration of 14 coaches from all areas of coaching have come together to provide wisdom and insight for those of you seeking "what's next"; those of you struggling to find your purpose, balance or spirituality in your life; and those of you who may be called to the coaching profession. You've read every one of the incredible and inspiring stories these coaches have had to tell. You've learned about their struggles and defeats and their perseverance and success. You've discovered the many tips and tools and sparks of ideas they've shared that can help people ignite the change they feel ready for in their life. Many became coaches because of some major life event that happened, others say coaching found them, and some have been doing it long before it was even called "life coaching." Some of these authors left jobs and careers to start a coaching practice from scratch, while others stayed within their companies and carved out a niche for themselves working with their teammates or higher level executives. There really is no limit to what you can envision and create for yourself when working with a life or business coach.

So…what's next for you? Ask yourself these questions.

"Why am I here?"
"What is my purpose?"
"Am I living someone else's dream?"

"Do I jump out of bed each day excited to be alive because I'm completely fulfilled in my work and personal life?"

Really think about your answers and if you're not happy with them, I so encourage you to explore working with a coach or enrolling in a coaching program. Sometimes we wonder if it's even possible to have the life we dream of, but the truth is that our time here is short and we can't afford to waste another moment wishing we had another career, another relationship or another life. Find your "what's next" now!

Dr. Diane Hayden
August, 2015

From the Clients

From Kelley Biskupiak's clients:

"Kelley defines herself as a 'space-creator,' creating space for women to become the best, most authentic version of themselves. But how she accomplishes this goes far beyond providing the tools and the time. Kelley has a unique ability to enable women to view people, circumstances, and events from a new angle, allowing them to discover their true potential, and inspiring them to make the changes necessary to reach their goals."

> ~ Lynn Ryan| Managing Director, Senior Portfolio Manager,
> Goodwin Capital Advisers, a Conning Company

"Kelley is a powerful coach. She creates a safe space for exploration and is courageous enough to challenge her clients to go after their dreams. She is passionate about education and empowering women to grow into the best versions of themselves, whatever that might be. If you are looking for clarity and the support to go after your dreams, I encourage you to talk to Kelley."

> ~ Dolores Hirschmann, CPCC, ACC,
> Contributor Creativ Magazine at [CREATIV]

From Deb Elbaums' Clients:

"Without any reservations, I would highly recommend the coaching services of Deb. She has been a tremendous help in my successful search for my first job back after ten years of caring for my children. As you can imagine it has been a difficult transition, there were times that I just wanted to suspend the search in frustration, but Deb always brought me back to the table with her own blend of "tough love." Now that I have that job I have had to reach out again to her for help with the adjustment to the working world. She has worked with me to problem solve, formulating an approach that gives me the confidence to go forward and advocate for myself and others successfully. I have nothing but the best to say about Deb and her services and endorse her practice wholeheartedly!"

~ D.K., Medical Social Worker, New Hampshire

"Deb has a gift for pushing you to think bigger, see things differently, and get past your own limiting beliefs that get in the way. I appreciate her knack for asking just the right question at just the right time, and her ability to stay with her clients every step of the way. She isn't afraid to ask the tough questions or to push you out of your comfort zone which is where growth and transformation occurs."

~ S.Y., Leadership Coach, Iowa

From Christel Autuori's clients:

"I was literally 'tanking'. Summer 2012 my energy level had plummeted. November, I spent 23 hours in the emergency room to investigate a cardiac crisis. I was frustrated with traditional medical choices but knew I needed help. Thankfully, I met Christel Autuori. Her pleasant and open manner was inviting and when she told me about Integrative Health Coaching I did not hesitate to request her as a coach. I was not familiar to this kind of relationship but felt an objective mind could help me focus my life into a more healthful and balanced direction. Christel has tremendous listening skills and used her knowledge to ask important questions that I had not been asking of myself. The Wheel of Health was an important visual tool that allowed me to see the whole picture of not just my health but why my life was so topsy-turvy. I had a chance to investigate where the imbalances

were and figure out why I was not working on making my dreams come true. This coaching approach kick-started me into making healthful integrative living Job #1. I positively recommend Christel as a Integrative Health Coach."

~ Cyndy, New Jersey

"The realization that it was okay to devote time to myself (and not 24/7 work) was not being selfish, but instead it was nurturing my being that made me a better and happier person. The discovery that I had this control was empowering and has allowed me to move forward with my personal and professional goals while leading a more balanced lifestyle. I could not have done this without your guidance, thank you for helping me to find myself!"

~ Wendy, Connecticut

From Christine Peterson's clients:

"Christine has helped me understand what the most important parts of my life are. No longer do I let months go by and wonder why I'm not happy and what to do about it. I know what the most important components are to me, and every day I focus on what makes me happy."

"The Wheel of Life was such an eye opener! It was so helpful to just take a few minutes and think objectively about how I am doing in each area of my life and where I want to focus to make me happy. Now my calendar is filled-ahead of time, with things that I WANT to do and that are important to me!"

From Diane Hayden's clients:

As a professional you bring incredible credentials, but as a person you bring so much more. Your passion, your presence, your personality, and your ambition.... they are all something to be admired. I just wanted you to know that in this life we sometimes do not realize the effect we have on others.

~ TM, Tampa, FL

Dr. Diane really got me motivated to pursue my passions and refocus on achieving my goals. This weekend was truly incredible and I feel so invigorated and passionate about taking life head on and seizing every opportunity to pursue my dreams.

I would strongly recommend bringing Dr. Diane back to work with our group again, she was able to revive our energy and bring us back into where we need and want to be. I feel so ready to pursue my dreams and I can't wait to see what the future will hold. Thank you for an amazing weekend, you are phenomenal at what you do.

~ AH, The Graduate Institute, Hartford, CT

From Andrew Miser's clients:

"Andy is a true professional and expert when it comes to helping couples get more out of life and truly understand and improve their relationship. My wife and I were privileged to be part of the pilot group for a weekend couples' retreat and came away with a much deeper understanding of our commitment to one another and tools to use for strengthening our love and respect for each other. Andy has a way of bringing out the best in people in a comforting environment and is great at listening, brainstorming and implementing positivity so that it can help others move forward in the right direction toward their goals. I would highly recommend Andy for his expertise." ~ Adam W., Framingham, Massachusetts

"Andy's Partners in Living course was just what we needed to learn where we had become disempowered in our marriage, focusing fully on our roles as parents and losing sight of the "us" in our relationship. Through Andy's committed listening and extraordinary coaching, we were not only able to see where our individual patterns of behavior had impacted our ability to dream, communicate and solve problems together, but also we were able to identify areas of our lives where we were aligned and operating in partnership without even realizing it. We both walked away with greater insight into how our own individual styles impact "us" and we gained invaluable tools to help us dream and create a vision for our future together. We also learned to accept where we are at right now and to not make that wrong. Life is a lot lighter and more enjoyable for our entire family thanks to Andy and the Partners in Living course. All couples could benefit from this program, and we highly recommend it if you are looking to enhance your partnership and live life to the fullest."

~ Lynne and Michael R., Plymouth, Massachusetts

From Mamek Charepoo's clients:

"Before I met Mamak, I had a very difficult time asking clients for money. I got to the point where I was deciding whether or not I should even continue my business. Then I met Mamak and everything changed. The sessions we had, the exercises she had me do, the questions she asked were incredibly thought provoking. She made me see myself in a new way, professionally and personally. Now, I have built my confidence and my business. I am charging what I am worth. My business is finally moving forward the way I had always envisioned. My advice before any woman starts her own business is to work with Mamak."

~ Ceylan Rowe, Owner and Founder Mommy's Business BFF

"Mamak's guidance and encouragement has helped me through resistance and to come into my power as a business woman. I have an increased confidence around my ability to connect with money. I have more structure, stronger boundaries and commitment to myself which are positively impacting all areas of my life. More people are being attracted to my business as I continue to grow by working consistently with Mamak." ~ Nicki Pakkala, Founder of Seed of Changes

From Louise Talotta's clients:

"Louise helped me deeply examine and think through my professional and personal goals. The key for me was to find that "intersection point" where personal & professional meet, where you can really find that work/life balance and be extremely happy while doing it. After working with Louise, I am truly enjoying the ride that life gives me each and every day!"

~ S. Saunders, New York Sales Executive

"The Governing board of the New Britain Industrial museum was thrilled to have Louise lead a workshop that focused on issues that were addressed in a completed Museum Assessment Program, (MAP). She led the board expertly toward clarifying many problematic areas, understanding the overall needs for prioritizing and she listened to many opinions while building upon the group's commonalities. We were able to capitalize on her excellent organizational abilities and talented

articulation of the steps necessary to formulate our strategic plan."

~ Board of Directors,
New Britain Industrial Museum, New Britain, CT

From Ellen Gilhooly's clients:

"Ellen's mentoring has been a great addition to my career development. Her energy has inspired me towards honest, strong leadership delivery. It means a great deal to be able to turn to her for advice, understanding, or just to be heard. Ellen is intuitive and to the point. Looking back I can clearly see the benefit I have gained from the time I have spent with her. I have a fresh direct approach that is in no small part to the time Ellen has spent mentoring me. It is rewarding to see the benefits at work. It is priceless to see how those same skills help my relationships outside of work."

"Ellen is an experienced leader who possesses excellent communication skills, is well organized, and can tackle complex issues that require a strong leader to help resolve. I worked with Ellen for 3 years and during that time there was never a situation, no matter how bad it got, that Ellen couldn't help us get through it. The thing I admire about her was in the toughest of times Ellen got even tougher, and would really pull people together, organize a game plan, and execute it to perfection. As a leader, I try to model certain behaviors from Ellen. Her strong resolve in handling tough situations with her organization and direction are what I strive to do every day."

From Tom Bohinc's clients:

"As an owner and executive it is unusual to find a resource that aligns all of our essential business domains in one package. Tom brings personal developmental and leadership development together with both a strategic and operational business perspective. It is a rare and valuable combination and helps focus our improvement across all time-scales. Working with Tom (and his Auorm team) has been a smart choice for us."

~ Joseph W, President and Founder, Roto Group LLC

"As a young professional working in the fast pace of new tech, I am not going to hesitate in recommending my coaching experience with Tom Bohinc to anyone with something exceptional to accomplish. With my coach, I set a path of achievement and personal fulfillment that has propelled me forward. I am very enthusiastic for my circumstance today and expectations for tomorrow. My recommendation is not only based on the result I've achieved, but on the experience itself and the character that I have built. The discussion, explorations and challenges from coaching led me to a new perspective that allows me to build sustainable successful practices. Anyone ready to maximize their potential using their strengths and passions will benefit from Auorm coaching."

~ Tyler Toohey, New York, NY

From Jeff Govoni's clients:

"Working with Jeff through the coaching process, I've identified the positive qualities I want to bring to every work situation. Identifying and developing practices that elevate these positives, and help me leave negatives behind, has given me a new sense of balance and awareness in my interactions across the organization. Jeff's inquisitive nature, persistence and his wide variety of interests and experiences have made it easy for us to connect and communicate around challenging concepts. I've learned a number of exercises and techniques which I've been able to use and benefit from in the day-to-day, while also focusing on the long term goal of being a better leader. After each session I truly feel better equipped to succeed and to help others find success. I've known Jeff for some years and eagerly recommend him to anyone seeking to develop new leadership tools or enhance their skills."

~ Joe McHugh, Customer Acquisition Manager,
Gardener's Supply Company

"I have been working on Executive Leadership with Jeff Govoni over the past year and appreciate and value the work I have been doing under his direction. I have been a CTO for over 15 years and have had 3-4 different executive coaches over this period. Having just started at Champlain College in July 2012 I did not think about additional executive leadership work. In a non-intuitive decision I chose to work with Jeff on my leadership style. My work with Jeff has been first and foremost reflective and historical. His work has helped me understand where my strengths and weaknesses come into play in my daily work. Jeff follows

his hunches and intuition with a set of frameworks that help with the personal reflection and with understanding the impact at work. Without reservation I recommend Jeff Govoni for executive leadership coaching."

~ Ted Laskaris, AVP Information Technology,
Champlain College, Burlington, VT

From Heidi Werther's clients:

"Working with Heidi, I was able to overcome my fear of trusting my inner voice and become my own Captain." ~ TC, Sales Executive

"Heidi is excellent at validating one's thinking and achievements and reminding clients where they are actually doing well as well as helping to raise thoughtful questions that lead to greater fulfillment." ~ CW, Sales Executive

"Working with you as a coach felt natural and touched on places I'm sensitive about and try to avoid, but when we got there I was happy you noticed me. I was touched, blown away, appreciative. Thank you for giving me recognition."

~ EB, Writer

From Jeanne Zuzel's clients:

"Because of her unique and complete approach to the change process, Jeanne helped me to understand that I could make changes in my life. She taught me how to become my very best by providing a full complement of therapies that were tailored to my individual needs. Jeanne's traditional medical and holistic training have been key to enhancing my core of self-awareness, healing and forward movement. I am fortunate and grateful to work with her. I came to Jeanne "a mess" and now my body and my heart are healing. Thank you Jeanne!"

~ L.H.-Norwich CT-2015

"Jeanne has a professional and personal approach. She has expertise in her field. Jeanne has proficiently lead me in the discovery of origins of some of life's sticking points and provides common sense options for making changes that have lead to healthier, happier living. Jeanne has an innate ability to connect with

those seeking healthy solutions to old or negative issues. I have learned so much from her; making positive changes in my own life that have now become habits and I know I will keep those good habits. Jeanne and I are now launching into a five year plan for myself to map out a creative and healthy vision complete with attainable goals that will encompass all my own intentions. I know that my relationship with Jeanne will continue to provide me the tools I need to remain healthy, whole and strong."   ~ Fawn Walker, Norwich, CT

From Lynnea Brinkerhoff's clients:

"Lynnea is one of the best coaches I have worked with. Her coaching involves the whole person: mind, body, spirit, emotion. When she invites her clients to self-reflect, we reflect on ALL levels: our logic, our feelings, and our energy and how they affect our physicality. She works in a continuous loop helping her clients build self-directed action plans that reflect her wise and affirming observations. Don't get me wrong, Lynnea's not 'easy.' She's not about pleasing you; she's in it to ensure you take yourself to the next level of personal efficacy."

~ Deborah Young,
Kroeger Organization Development Manager
at Integration Partners

"I have had the great pleasure in being coached by Lynnea Brinkerhoff. I felt comfortable and at ease with Lynnea's relaxed approach from the start. It felt like I have known her for a long time and it was like talking to an old friend. At the same time she asks tough questions that helped me resolve some critical business and personal issues. Through her coaching and insights I was able to transcend my current situations and become more effective, efficient, relaxed and open to more creative ideas. My overall quality of life has benefited from knowing her and I'm happy to call her a friend."

~ David Gilman,
Senior Customer Relations Development Manager,
Kaiser Permanente

155

Suggested Reading & Resources

Books:

All Day Long by Jeffrey Brantley MD and Wendy Millstine.

Ask and it is Given: Learning to Manifest Your Desires by Esther and Jerry Hicks. Medicine Cards: The Discovery of Power Through the Ways of Animals by J Sams and D Carson.

Beyond the myth of marital happiness: How embracing the virtues of loyalty, generosity, justice and courage can strengthen your relationship by B. Fowers.

Changing on the Job, Developing Leaders for a Complex World by Jennifer Garvey Berger.

Co-Active Coaching, third edition, by Henry Kimsey-House, Karen Kimsey-House, Phillip Sandahl, and Laura Whitworth.

Dare, Dream, Do: Remarkable Thing Happen When You Dare To Dream by Whitney Johnson.

Daring Greatly: How the Courage to Be Vulnerable Transforms the Way We Live, Love, Parent, and Lead by Brene Brown.

Difficult Conversations: How to Discuss What Matters Most by Douglas Stone, Bruce Patton and Sheila Heen.

Executive Coaching by Catherine Fitzgerald and Jennifer Garvey Berger.

Five Good Minutes: 100 Morning Practices to Help You Stay Calm by Jeffry Brantley and Wendy Millstine.

Give and Take by Adam Grant.

Good to Great by Jim Collins.

Heal Your Body, by Louise Hay.

Integrative Health Rules: A Simple Guide to Healthy Living by Dr. Jim Nicolai.

Leadership and Self-Deception: Getting out of the Box by The Arbinger Institute.

Learned optimism: How to change your mind and your life by Martin Seligman.

Marriage, a history: How love conquered marriage by S. Coontz.

Mindset: The New Psychology of Success: How We Can Fulfill our Potential by Carol S. Dweck, Ph.D.

New Directions for Rational Emotive Behavioral Therapy: Overcoming Destructive Beliefs, Feelings and Behaviors by Albert Ellis.

Nurse Coaching: Integrative Approaches for Health and Wellbeing by Barbara Dossey.

Play to Win, Choosing Growth Over Fear in Work and Life by Larry Wilson and Hersch Wilson.

Radical Acceptance: Embracing Life with the heart of a Buddha by Tara Brach PHD.

Sacred Contracts by Carolyn Myss.

Six Thinking Hats by Edward De Bono.

Start with Why by Simon Sinek.

Strengths Based Leadership by Tom Rath and Barry Conichie.

Sustainable Wellness: An Integrative Approach to Transform Your Mind, Body, and Spirit by Matt Mumber, MD and Heather Reed.

Take Back your Marriage: Sticking together in a world that pulls us apart by W.J. Doherty.

Taming Your Gremlin by Rick Carson.

The Art of Extreme Self-Care: Transform Your Life One Month at a Time by Cheryl Richardson.

The Book of Awakening, by Mark Nepo.

The Fire Starter Sessions, by Danielle LaPorte.

The Fire Starter Sessions: A Soulful and Practical Guide to Creating Success on Your Own Terms by Danielle LaPorte.

The Gifts of Imperfection: Let Go of Who You Think You're Supposed to Be and Embrace Who You Are by Brene Brown.

The Heart Aroused by David Whyte.

The Marriage-Go-Round: The state of marriage and family in America today by A.J. Cherlin.

The Miracle of Mindfulness by Thich Nhat Hanh.

The Mother's Guide to Self-Renewal: How to Reclaim, Rejuvenate and Re-Balance Your Life by Renee Peterson Trudeau.

The Partnership Marriage: Creating the Life You Love...Together by Andrew Miser.

The Power of Commitment: A guide to lifelong love by S.M. Stanley.

The Power of Intention by Dr. Wayne W. Dyer.

The Seven Stages of Marriage: Laughter, intimacy, and passion, today, tomorrow, and forever by S. Harrar & R. DeMaria.

Think and Grow Rich, by Napolean Hill.

Thrive: The Third Metric to Redefining Success and Creating a Life of Well-Being, Wisdom, and Wonder by Arianna Huffington.

Walk Out Walk On, A learning journey into communities by Margaret Wheatley, Deborah Frieze.

What Color is Your Parachute? by Richard N. Bolles.

Why marriages succeed or fail: And how you can make yours last by J.M. Gottman.

You Are Oprah - Igniting the Fires of Greatness by Howard Glasser and Melissa Lynn Block.

Websites:

http://www.authentichappiness.org/: All about positivity; offers articles, news, questionnaires, positivity books, etc.

http://www.centreforconfidence.co.uk/pp/overview. The psychology of being positive.

http://www.individualdifferences.com/node/2. Building resilience for success in work and life.

http://www.newincites.com. INCITE Health and Wellness Center.

http://www.zentangle.com. A unique way to relax through art and sketching.

Assessments:

http://www.finestramedia.com/resiliency/(an interactive on-line course by Seibert)

http://www.iptv.org/video/detail.cfm/5840/temo_20100104_happiness_resilience_connecting (From This emotional life, PBS:several video options)

http://leadershipcircle.com/: The Leadership Circle is an innovative and unique measure of your leadership strength and maturity which Auorm uses as part of its practices.

http://positiveintelligence.com/assessments/: (Shirzad Chamine: Understanding your inner saboteur)

http://www.ppc.sas.upenn.edu/ppquestionnaires.htm (Seligman: Positive Psychology Center questionnaires – gratitude, hope, mindful attention, curiosity, well-being, etc…)

http://www.resiliencyinitiatives.ca (Hammond: Resiliency Model and Frameworks: The "Assessing Developmental Strengths" and "Core Competencies" frameworks are used to assess resiliency, build capacity, and shift paradigms toward Strengths-Based culture)

http://www.yogananda-srf.org/, or http://shambhala.org/: Resources or building awareness of mindfulness and mediation in the eastern tradition. Having the ability to stay in the present and to be in creative relationships to your past and future are leadership strengths.

Index

163

About the Authors

Kelley Biskupiak, MA, CPCC

Uniquely qualified founder and owner of Be You Bravely, Kelley Biskupiak launched this personal and professional coaching firm because she believes strongly in empowering women and families to lead and live fulfilling lives. Kelley works with clients to get clarity in the chaos and develop a goal-based purpose plan that can be implemented into their life. The result is more balance and fulfillment and a life lived with purpose and meaning. As a wife, mother of three boys, business owner, Workshop Facilitator, Motivational Speaker, Blogger, Author and Educational Leadership Coach Kelley has learned to "walk this talk" in her own life. Kelley holds a BA in both Communication Studies and Education, from the University of Rhode Island as well as a Masters Degree in Literacy from Pace University. She has worked in the educational arena in many capacities ranging from teaching, administration and consulting. She currently works for Leadership Greater Hartford as an Educational Leadership Coach and is Principal at her coaching practice, Be You Bravely. Kelley is also host and facilitator for a monthly workshop series for women titled, "Ladies Night Out." Kelley was trained as a Co-Active Coach at the esteemed Coaches Training Institute (CTI) and holds a CPCC certification. She is a member of the International Coaching Federation (ICF). Kelley Biskupiak, MA, CPCC, 203-216-3956, beyoubravely.com, kelley@beyoubravely.com.

Deborah Elbaum, MD, CPCC, ACC

Deb Elbaum, MD, CPCC, ACC, is a certified career and life coach who helps her clients get clear about their choices, take action, trust their decisions, and create intentional change. She works with professionals who are navigating career transition, women who are reentering the workforce, and individuals who are seeking more purpose in life. Before becoming a coach, Deb worked as a physician and medical writer. In addition to being a coach, author, speaker, wife, and mother, Deb is a Founding Fellow at the Harvard Medical School-affiliated Institute of Coaching, a nonprofit organization dedicated to furthering quality research on coaching. She is also a coach and workshop presenter for the Institute for Career Transitions at Massachusetts Institute of Technology, an organization supporting long-term unemployed individuals. Her bachelor's degree in psychology is from Harvard University, her MD degree is from the University of Pennsylvania, and her coaching certification is from the Coaches Training Institute. She lives in Massachusetts with her husband and three children. For more information, visit www.DebElbaum.com or email Deb@DebElbaum.com

Christel Autuori, RDH, RYT, MA

Christel Autuori believes in a multidimensional, holistic, interactive, and preventive approach to health and vitality, and is passionate about helping people create, maintain, and sustain optimal health and happiness. She is the founder and owner of Integrative Health of Connecticut, providing integrative health coaching and holistic stress management services as well as yoga instruction and workshops to individuals, groups, and organizations. She is a professional speaker, author, educator, consultant, and practitioner. Christel is a partner and guide for her clients as they paint a picture of optimal health and what it means to them and for their life. Together they explore and examine areas of imbalance and dis-ease, and create and implement a realistic, practical, personalized plan for change—Positive HealthStyles—with a holistic approach to health and happiness in life. Christel is a registered dental hygienist, registered yoga teacher, certified Reiki master, certified holistic stress management instructor, and a certified integrative health coach. She has a Masters' degree in Integrative Health and Healing and is a graduate of the Integrative Health Coach Professional Training program at Duke Integrative Medicine. She is a founder of the Global Integrative Health Coaching Alliance (www.gihca. org) and an adjunct faculty member at Western Connecticut State University. Christel Autuori, RDH, RYT, MA, CICH, 203.788.0647, www.integrativehealthct.com.

Christine Bilotti Peterson, MBA

Christine Bilotti Peterson has over 20 years of experience in the financial services industry where she has held a variety of Human Resource leadership positions. Christine earned her undergraduate degree in Marketing and Communications at Central Connecticut State University and completed her MBA at The Lally School of Business at Rensselaer Polytechnic University. Christine became a Certified Executive Coach in 2013 through the International Coaching Federation. She passionately enjoys working with clients to create their aspirational goals and achieve them both personally and professionally. For more information or assistance to help you reach your goals, live life more authentically, and create the life you want to live, please contact, Executive Coach: Christine Bilotti Peterson at cbpeterson@me.com.

Diane Hayden, PhD

Dr. Diane Hayden is the owner and publisher of Natural Nutmeg Magazine, Essential Living Maine Magazine and Nutmeg Creative Media. She is a speaker, writer and workshop facilitator. She holds a B.S. in Marketing from the University of Connecticut, a Ph.D. in Exercise Physiology from the University of Maryland and is an Empowerment Life Coach. For 20 years, her work has focused on inspiring individuals to learn about the power of thought and emotion and how it shapes their lives. Her passion centers on helping even just one person navigate the dating scene and find the perfect partner with whom they can share their life You can learn more about her online at http:naturalnutmeg.com/category/where-is-dr-di-travel or http:drdianehayden.com.

Andrew L. Miser, PhD, CPCC, PCC

Andrew Miser is a professional coach who specializes in coaching baby boomer couples in designing a shared life of passion, fulfillment and contribution. Andy recently published a book entitled The Partnership Marriage: Creating the Life You Love...Together. Working with couples individually and in groups, he supports couples in clarifying what's important to them, creating a shared vision of the future and taking action to fulfill the future they've envisioned. Andy has developed an innovative coaching curriculum designed for couples committed to bringing greater partnership into their lives. Prior to focusing exclusively on partnership marriage, Andy was a psychologist and marriage and family therapist in private practice in Hartford, Connecticut. He has a Ph.D. in Developmental Psychology from The University of Connecticut. Andy was trained as a Co-active Coach through the Coaches Training Institute (CTI) and is currently on the faculty of CTI. Andy is a member of the American Psychological Association, a Clinical Member of the American Association of Marriage and Family Therapy and a Professional Certified Coach with the International Coach Federation. Andy lives in Boston with his wife and partner, Martha. They've been married for 40 years. Andrew L. Miser, Ph.D., CPCC, PCC, 617-942-2757, andy@thepartnershipmarriage.com.

Mamak Charepoo, MM, MFA, NHA® Advanced Trainer, SMA® Certified Coach

Mamak Charepoo believes that everyone has the right to feel safe to flourish. Her own journey in shifting money beliefs that were sabotaging her success and prosperity has inspired her to work with organizations, groups and individuals in promoting and presenting the value of their product and services, having money conversations with ease, and creating service structures that are aligned with their values and goals. Mamak has a Master of Fine Arts from Arizona State University and a Master of Music from Carnegie Mellon University. She has been a collaborator, teacher, trainer, and speaker in her music, children's class coordinator and coaching careers. She has been interviewed on Powerful Women Revealed radio and PACTV, and has been highlighted by popular HBR blogger, Whitney Johnson's Dare to Dream blog. She is a Nurtured Heart Approach® Advanced Trainer, and Sacred Money Archetype® Certified Coach. She is a member of IAWC and Pod Leader for Believe Inspire Grow. Mamak Charepoo, MM, MFA, NHA® Advanced Trainer, SMA® Certified Coach, 617-959-9581, www.charepoocoaching.com.

Louise Talotta, CPC

Louise Talotta, CPC, of BridgeLight Coaching, LLC is a certified life and business coach with over 30 years of experience in health care and Fortune 100 companies. Her long professional career allowed her to work with many leaders and employees who navigated obstacles and strove to make a difference in their work while trying to balance full and busy lives. Her coaching business was born from the passion of helping people evaluate and reframe their perspectives to expand into their possibilities. She is accredited by the International Coaching Academy, ICA, for life and business coaching. Her educational background at the University of Connecticut includes a bachelor's degree with honors in organizational management and a Business Mastery certification. Her education and background in Human Resources, leadership and strategic planning brings expertise and insights for her clients through in-person, telephone or online sessions. By bringing intuitive coaching and people skills to her clients, they are supported to reach amazing goals. http://www.bridgelightcoaching.com, bridgelightcoaching@yahoo.com.

Ellen Gilhooly, RP, MPC

Ellen Gilhooly's experience includes five years of Body Center Gestalt training from the Hartford Family Institute and ten years' experience as a Master Reiki Practitioner. She recently completed a Master's Degree in Pastoral Counseling. For the last 26 years, Ellen worked for a fortune 500 Healthcare Company as a Senior Director managing three technology teams as well as acting as a Chief of Staff for an Executive Director. During her career, she had the opportunity to hold positions in Human Resources and mentored several managers to enhance their leadership skills. Ellen created Partners In Spirit to help people see through their chaos in order to discover and create a clear vision for their lives. She helps guide and support people to make each day a blessing and to embrace their individual life force. Most importantly, she helps an individual identify the times when they are operating more from their ego which stifles their inner spirit. Our ego is to help us to survive, not thrive. Ellen believes most people want to thrive not just survive. Ellen Gilhooly, partnersinspirit@yahoo.com.

Tom Bohinc, MBA, CPCC

Tom Bohinc is an expert in creative leadership and both personal and team peformance. His mission is to help each of us recognize our own leadership potential and to create an impact. Tom's passion around this has grown from over thirty years leading on the front-lines of organizations, from start-ups to global giants. He is fueled both by the energy of high-performing teams and the tragedy of under-performing ones. He has led innovations that changed industries, and witnessed too many that were not-as-successful. In all these cases the presence or absence of 'creative leadership factors' made the difference. Tom never tires of the opportunity to discover strengths in clients and their potential to thrive and to affect their world. Tom brings consulting and executive-level business experience in companies leading in their industries. He holds an MBA from The Weatherhead School at Case Western Reserve University. Tom also holds a CPCC certification as a Co-Active Coach from the esteemed Coaches Training Institute (CTI) as well as certification with The Leadership Circle. He is a member of the International Coaching Federation (ICF). He is the founder of the Auorm Group. He would love to hear from you at tom@auorm.com

Jeff Govoni, PCC

Jeff Govoni is founder and principal of Springtide Leadership Development. His mission is to improve the way we work and live by helping professionals of any level see with new eyes, feel with greater understanding, and discover their intrinsic capacity to lead. By helping individuals and groups notice with clarity how and who they are now, he develops their capacity to identify who and how they want to be in the future and together develops practices to get there. Jeff's approach is to guide clients through an exploration of their assessments, personal beliefs and thought patterns that drive their range of options. Through appreciative inquiry, personal reflections and practices and constructive input, Springtide Leadership clients develop the capacity to expand their range of options and chart a new course to a more desirable and effective future. Since obtaining his credential in Leadership Coaching from Georgetown University's prestigious Center for Transformational Leadership, Jeff has been working with senior leaders in the public and private sectors in Vermont, Virginia, Washington D.C., Central and South America and Canada. Jeff has worked with individuals and teams in both a coaching and in a facilitation capacity. jeffgovoni@gmail.com, www.springtideleadership.com.

Heidi Werther, MS, CPCC, ACC

Passionate about empowering others in transition, certified professional coach, mediator, facilitator and consultant, Heidi Werther works with individuals, families and organizations in transition inspiring them to embrace changes that fuel constructive results. Her 25 years in the business world, along with her personal experiences, defined her coaching niche working with individuals looking for the next step in their career or looking to completely reinvent themselves; entrepreneurs or small business owners requiring a guide as they define or expand their business; people looking for more in their relationships and parents looking to improve their co-parenting skills. An expert in her field through her work achievements, academic studies, and personal life experiences, Heidi listens to her clients, helps them to clarify their purpose, communicate their dreams, desires and goals, and challenges them to take action allowing them to move forward in the direction they choose. She believes her clients have the answers within. Heidi obtained her Master of Science, Mediation and Applied Conflict Studies from Champlain College, and her coaching certification, Certified Professional Co-active Coach (CPCC), from the highly acclaimed Coaches Training Institute (CTI). She is an active member of the International Coaching Federation (ICF) and its New England Chapter, as well as several mediation associations and facilitator's groups. Heidi is the proud parent of two wonderful young men who opened her eyes to curiosity, the true meaning of passion, and the benefits of taking risks. Heidi Werther, MS, CPCC, ACC, 617.365.9550, heidiwerther.com.

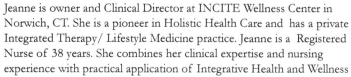

Jeanne C. Zuzel RN, MA

Jeanne is owner and Clinical Director at INCITE Wellness Center in Norwich, CT. She is a pioneer in Holistic Health Care and has a private Integrated Therapy/ Lifestyle Medicine practice. Jeanne is a Registered Nurse of 38 years. She combines her clinical expertise and nursing experience with practical application of Integrative Health and Wellness concepts. Jeanne believes that change is a process and NOT an event...She supports her clients through all phases of the change process. This invites her clients and students to experience the opportunity for ultimate personal growth, learning and healing. Jeanne is an Adjunct Professor at local colleges and enhances her practice by offering sessions and seminars in Healing Touch, Expressive Art, Holistic Health, Wellness and Stress management. Jeanne is a Certified Healing Touch Practitioner and Instructor. She has a Master's degree in Integrative Health and Healing, A Certificate in Expressive art therapy and is a board certified Nurse Health & Wellness Coach. Jeanne is available to support your journey. You may contact her via email: incite.learn@yahoo.com, or telephone 860-889-4690. Visit her website: www.newincites.com.

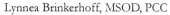

Lynnea Brinkerhoff, MSOD, PCC

Lynnea Brinkerhoff, founder of Radical Nourishment™, is a Board Certified Executive and Wellness Coach, International Coach Federation PCC level and Board member. She brings 25 years of experience in operational and strategic roles in hospitality, healthcare and wilderness-based education to her work with leaders in transition who are seeking greater results, satisfaction and resilience in life and purpose-driven work. Co-founder of the StressSquad™ and the first Eco-therapy program on the east coast, Lynnea is a seasoned practitioner of several integrative health methods and continues to seek remedies for modern day maladies. She also serves as Disaster Chaplain for NYC. She has authored works in resilience, neuroscience of leadership, organizational alignment, equine assisted coaching and collaborative strategic planning. Lynnea has an ability to put people at ease, to sense into their unspoken aspirations and fears and, using a strengths-based, no-nonsense approach, turning them into concrete operational results. Lynnea invites people to see their repeating patterns, the needs of their stakeholders and to choose the most effective path forward to accomplish their mission. She enjoys cayenne pepper and swims in the ocean on New Year's Day for the last 25 years. www.Lynneabrinkerhoff.com, www.EponaDevi.com, www.TriStateSoulfulCeremonies.com, Lynneabrink@gmail.com.

Readers Notes